The WHITEHALL Effect

**How Whitehall became the enemy of
great public services and what
we can do about it**

John Seddon

Foreword by
Lord Victor Adebowale

Published in this first edition in 2014 by:
Triarchy Press
Station Offices
Axminster
Devon
EX13 5PF
England

+44 (0)1297 631456
info@triarchypress.net
www.triarchypress.net

A catalogue record for this book is available from the British Library.

Cover illustration by Gerald Scarfe

ISBN: 978-1-909470-47-7

Acknowledgements

Brendan O'Donovan, Vanguard's head of research, clarified and corrected my memory during the writing and prepared the notes that accompany the text. His work, as ever, was invaluable to me. Simon Caulkin (www.simoncaulkin.com), award-winning management journalist, management thinker and friend gave life, clarity and style to my prose; the book is better for it. Finally, without our clients — both private-and public-sector — and Vanguard consultants, the practical and theoretical content would not have been possible.

Contents

Foreword

By Lord Victor O. Adebowale, CBE, MA
CEO, Turning Point, Health and social care
Chair, Collaborate

It has been accepted for far too long, in the face of clear evidence to the contrary, that the machine age is a good thing in and of itself, and that applying the principles of efficient factory management to human-facing public services is also a good thing.

The truths set out eloquently and with ample evidence and anecdote in this book clearly show that public services don't work that way. (I prefer to call them 'services-to-the-public', because it's not about who provides them, it's about the value such services bring to the lives of individuals and communities we all hold dear.) The book shows that the top-down design and organisation of services-to-the-public doesn't work. It also shows that the wholesale transfer of systems designed for running factories (including outsourcing and separate back- and front-offices) to services that deal with human beings doesn't work either.

John Seddon's simple exposition of the different motivations of front-office, customer-facing operations as opposed to back-office, administrative processes exposes the obvious fallacy in the assumption that this is the best way of organising services designed to meet human needs. The example he gives of Swale Borough Council's housing benefits department clearly highlights the size of the problem and the scale of the opportunity.

This isn't John Seddon's first foray into the world of public service design and delivery. His book *Freedom from Command and Control* was a manifesto for just doing things better that spoke clearly of the waste of human potential caused by bureaucracies more interested in power and position than in the value and values that actually make a difference to the customer of any service — public or private.

Now, in *The Whitehall Effect*, he takes a clear-eyed view of the causes of the disease that I have talked about time and time again in my descriptions of too many services-to-the-public: that disease is failure demand. Behind the idea of a crisis in our public services caused by mounting demand is the reality that the crisis is not generated by 'demanding customers' but by the failure of services to deal effectively with the customer first time round. This creates the need for more contacts, more explanation and more activity – all forms of failure demand that are of 'negative value' to the customer, the service and certainly the tax payer.

What becomes clear throughout this book is that our services-to-the-public need redesigning not cutting and that they simply cannot be redesigned without a deep understanding of the citizen/customer at the heart of the design process. Seddon sets out what this means in practice and invites service providers to ask some simple questions of the service experience – to take a walk in the shoes of the user of their service. I have done this on many occasions and often shocked myself at the massive difference between the intention of the service and the actual effect it has on the lives of individuals, both customers and employees. Just as shocking is the waste of talent, ideas and experience that failure demand generates at huge cost to the public purse.

It doesn't have to be this way and in this book Seddon sets out the principles and practice of how public services could empower citizens, could be exciting (yes exciting) to deliver and could genuinely add value to the lives of the public who pay for them. Seddon makes the clear distinction between thinking that you know and actually knowing, by taking the trouble to engage with the experience of the customer.

I happened to have listened to the interview with the BBC's Peter Day that Seddon refers to in Chapter 7. In it, Seddon pointed out in his usual blunt and evidenced-based way just how little many managers know about demand in customer terms — much to the astonishment of his interviewer. At the time I could only agree with Seddon because I too have fallen into the trap of thinking about volume of demand rather than type of demand as well as the trap of thinking that by focusing on reducing cost I will improve services. Traps are pretty easy to fall into. In fact there are many consultancies that will help you — with the best of intentions — design the trap, step into it and turn the screw in complete ignorance of the fact that, if you want to improve services, focusing on cost simply increases your costs. The volume trap is even easier to fall into and it's worth taking a paragraph from the book that makes my point for me:

> Payment for volume of activity is a common and fundamental error in outsourcing contracts. It incentivises increased activity, the last thing that is wanted in any service, least of all one that consumes public funds. It doesn't take a genius to work out that under a volume-based contract, the more failure demand the system generates, the better it is for the outsource provider. The worse the service from the customer's point of view, the greater the benefit to the provider's revenues.

Enough said. I guess this brings into focus one underlying theme of this book, which is that the current paradigm is difficult to shift because so many people benefit from its failure to actually deliver. There are billions at stake, effectively tied up in doing the wrong thing. What this book sets out, in a way that will make uncomfortable but necessary reading for some people in Whitehall, is that we waste money and people on what John Seddon calls 'pleasant dreams' — fantasies based on misnomers, vested interests and received wisdom — instead of taking the trouble to look at what actually works, the reality of customer experience and the dangers inherent in failure demand.

~~~

John Seddon's forensic eye is sobering and brings clarity and some sense of empowerment for those like myself who believe passionately in delivering better services-to-the-public.

In *The Whitehall Effect* he patiently presents us with the truth about what lies *behind* the daily frustrations, denial of service and sheer waste that is too often the citizen's experience of public services. He gives us a clear technical understanding of the issues and addresses head-on the question of leadership and the work that needs to be done by those who decide the shape of those services on behalf of us all.

Most truths that I have come across tend to have the look of the obvious about them and this book contains truths that many, like me, will find self-evident.

~~~

The Whitehall Effect could not have been published at a better time. As I write, we are seven months away from a general election in which the economy will loom large as the dark cloud under which the next administration will have to work. More austerity, more cuts, the search for more for less — much less — will be the challenge Whitehall will face. In terms of cutting costs and reducing expenditure, the low hanging fruit have already been picked (though not necessarily in the right way) and we are now into cutting into the tree itself. At such a time, doing what we have always done will simply generate more of the same results: more failure demand, increasing costs, decreasing value and vested interests silent about the truth of all this.

We need a new paradigm that puts the citizen/customer first, drives value into the lives of recipients and costs less, not just because we have cut costs but because we have improved value. This is the challenge behind what needs to be our 21st-century vision for services-to-the-public. *The Whitehall Effect* sets out the way we might deliver better services. It should be required reading for anyone who delivers a service to the public.

3rd October 2014

Introduction

Politicians don't know much about management.

In the last 30 years expenditure on public services has rocketed from £150bn in 1985 to an eye-watering £674bn in 2013. Spending has trebled since 1990-1991 and doubled since 2000-2001[1]. By any standards, this is a dramatic increase in costs in a period when politicians have chosen to place themselves at the helm of public-sector reform — all prime ministers since Margaret Thatcher have declared public-sector reform to be their greatest domestic priority. Beginning with Thatcher's administration, every successive government has actively intervened with a range of specific measures – all of them intended to improve public services and reduce costs. Yet claims that any actual improvements have been achieved are, to say the least, doubtful and not a week passes without news of costly catastrophes.

It is the same story if we look at it through the lens of productivity. The Institute for Fiscal Studies has estimated that if levels of productivity in 2007 had been the same as in 1997 it would have released £42bn[2]. Greg Clark MP, then Treasury minister, reported in 2012 that if the public sector had kept pace with average private-sector productivity between 1997 and 2007 then it would be nearly a quarter more productive[3].

Clearly, whichever way we look at it, reform isn't working. Something isn't right.

However, these statistics are high-level, telling us something about the 'what', but nothing about 'why'. To understand more about 'why', we have to get down into the detail, to see what reform has meant in practice.

When we do that, it gives a very different slant to the story the politicians like to tell us. Their narrative is that demand for public services is rising — which it is, but not for the reasons they think. Politicians point the finger at an ageing population, with more complex problems, and rising expectations of citizens who have become 'customers'. But in fact demand is rising because public services don't work — they don't serve.

The lengthening queues forming at the front doors into health, social care, benefits, housing, planning and other services are caused by the failure of the services to meet people's needs. I call this failure demand, which in public services can account for as much as 80% of the total demand volume; failure demand is caused by the way public services are designed and managed. It will not be a surprise that benefits and other offices these days feature notices to the effect that abusive behaviour will not be tolerated, but there seems little understanding that people are bound to become abusive if they feel frustrated, ignored and can't get their problem solved.

What is the problem with the way we have designed and managed public services? A major one, in simple terms, is that they have been industrialised. That is, computers have been used to apply to services concepts that were devised for mass-production factories a century ago. In Part 1 I shall delve into the detail of industrialisation to show why the conventional solutions — call centres, back offices, shared services, outsourcing and IT-led change — all lead to service failure. I shall expose the myth of scale, the mantra 'bigger is better' that has dominated public-sector reform. The only scale is the scale of failure.

Another way to demonstrate the causes of failure is to show how better services at much lower costs are achieved through abandoning scale thinking, and that is the purpose of Part 2. Instead of being industrialised, alienating and unresponsive, good services are attuned and sensitive to people's needs. This exposes the fundamental flaw in industrial, 'bigger is better' thinking; trying to drive down costs actually drives costs up. The better focus — managing value — drives costs down, and by surprisingly large amounts.

Managing value is foreign territory for politicians and managers. It requires a profound shift in thinking; many of the ideas run completely against the grain. 'Getting it' is to cross a Rubicon and the best — only — way to achieve that is for managers to study and learn for themselves that conventional ideas are only that, conventional; and conventional is not the same as useful.

The most challenging ideas — that targets, inspection, regulation and incentives are part of the problem and not the solution — are the focus of Part 3. Part 3 also includes an explanation of the big lever for change and improvement, managing the system not the people. This is the starting-place for designing and managing services that work.

Having covered the theory, in Part 4 I shall discuss some of the current fads in public-sector reform. Some, like 'choice' are ideological; some, like 'managing demand', 'nudge' and 'lean' are based on bad theory; some, like IT-led change have no theory at all. Politicians pursue fads because they are plausible and fit their narrative, the stories they like to tell about reform; but these things, like industrialisation, only serve to make public services worse or, at best, detract from the opportunity at hand.

Because the other side of the coin is that the opportunity is nothing short of breathtaking. We can undo the costly debacle that has occurred in the name of public sector reform — but only if we firstly change Whitehall. In Part 5 I describe why politicians should be more circumspect about economic theories, how Whitehall is systemically incapable of listening to and acting on evidence and how it needs to change its ways if the mistakes of the last 35 years are to be avoided and the profound opportunity realised.

Politicians are not well disposed to admitting they are wrong. But they must get over that if we are to achieve what we all want — better public services at much lower costs. If politicians find the evidence uncomfortable, I hope they will be encouraged to reflect by the electorate who, I hope, will use this book as a source for questions that should be put to them. Simple ones are good for starters, like: 'Do you accept that public-sector reform hasn't worked?' and 'What do you believe to be the reasons?' Armed with the arguments and evidence contained herein, whatever the reply, supplementary questions will only be harder. If politicians learn that votes are dependent on showing a better understanding we can anticipate that they might start to talk the talk, and some may even start to understand.

But before we get to the main arguments I need to review how politicians have thought about public sector reform, from Margaret Thatcher through to the current coalition. What is perhaps surprising is that there is a political consensus; only disturbing because it is wrong. Politicians don't know much about management — and much of what they do know is wrong.

Chapter 1: Prelude

Ministers enter management

Back in the day, public administration (rather than 'public service') was something conceived as a Weberian bureaucracy, honest and fair, funded by the state, treating all citizens alike, governed by clear procedures and rules, where role and position in the civil-service hierarchy conferred the power to behave within a clear legal framework. As the economy grew, public services grew with it. With the advent of an economic shock in the early 1970s, public-sector reform began to be a political priority. Public services were increasing demands on national resources, something that was perceived as no longer affordable in the long term.

People argued — as they do today — that expenditure was out of control because of statutory entitlements to benefits and services. Escalating cost was also attributed to inefficient ways of working. There had been costly debacles, for example ballistic missiles forecast to cost £50m but eventually totalling over £300m (in fact a trivial waste compared to recent IT-related failures). Concorde, dubbed the flying white elephant, only took off after consuming well over a billion from the public purse[1]. Many people argued that the cause was civil service incompetence in managing resources.

Margaret Thatcher (1997-1990)

Into this developing maelstrom entered Margaret Thatcher, who, it has to be said, mixing metaphors, stirred up the hornet's nest by taking the most resolutely negative view of the public sector of all British prime ministers. She rejected as "a socialist ratchet"[2] the post-war consensus of the state as a benevolent provider of public services, was alarmist about the costs associated with universal welfare benefits and, inspired by the economist Friedrich Hayek, argued that any increase in the role of the state would destroy free enterprise by draining resources away from wealth-creating activities[3].

Thatcher pointed to growing numbers of "wealth-consuming" public sector jobs and believed civil servants acted in their own "producer" interests ("we pay through the nose in prices and taxes and take what we are given"[4]). She scorned public-sector leaders for being no good — otherwise they'd be working for the private sector[5] — and took the view that where public services couldn't be privatised, the preferred option, their managers should take lessons from the private sector. This was at a time when private-sector companies had begun to construct call centres and centralise 'back-office' activities in pursuit of the assumed benefits of economies of scale.

Thatcher reckoned that private-sector service organisations' focus on customer service would bring a breath of fresh air to cumbersome public-service bureaucracies, making them more citizen-centric. Following Hayek, Thatcher introduced the concept of choice, treating users of public services as customers. If people weren't free to choose what they consumed, she reasoned, power would inevitably accrue to politicians, bureaucrats and providers of services instead[6].

The central driver was expenditure: in other words cost. 'Doing more with less' became a mantra. The public sector was encouraged to adopt 'proven' private-sector methods, to compete on price, to deal with labour indiscipline, to fight trade unions, to develop stronger financial controls and to employ information technology to drive down service costs.

Within days of taking office Thatcher appointed Derek Rayner, then joint managing director of Marks & Spencer, to spearhead a drive against waste and inefficiency. In her first year she established an 'Efficiency Unit' which brought government departments before her to be scrutinised for ways of saving money.

In 1980 came Compulsory Competitive Tendering (CCT). CCT opened up public-sector contracts to private companies by obliging local authorities to put services out to tender. Initially CCT was limited to highways and buildings maintenance and minor building work, but in 1988 it was extended to include refuse collection, street and building cleaning, schools and welfare catering, meals-on-wheels, and grounds and vehicle maintenance. From 1989 CCT also covered council sports and leisure services. In 1992 it was broadened further to include professional, financial and technical services, and then in 1993 it was extended to many of the activities in housing management.

The intervention that was to have the most profound effect on public-service operations under successive governments was the creation of the Audit Commission in 1983. Michael Heseltine, a secretary of state in Thatcher's cabinet who had made his name (and money) as a private-sector media baron, was the architect. The idea was to replace district audit functions, whose purpose had been to audit financial probity, with an organisation that would not only audit spending but would also evaluate public-sector organisations' operational performance. Audit now had the remit to roam as consultants in performance improvement; perhaps not coincidentally, the Commission's first two chief executives had previously worked for McKinsey.

In 1988 Thatcher proposed turning half of Whitehall into 'agencies' with the aim of freeing government departments from central control to focus on 'delivery' against frameworks including policy, targets and outcomes, agreed with ministers. While ostensibly free to deliver, the new agencies were to be subjected to a "constant and sustained pressure for improvement"[7]. The waves of agency creation continued right through the 1990s. Within a decade three-quarters of civil servants were employed in agencies.

In 1989 Thatcher turned her attention to the health service. In 10 years her government had increased health spending by 40%[8], yet in her view the NHS remained an inefficient and patient-unfriendly monolith. This could not continue — the more so as demand for health services would only increase as the population aged. To cope with this, she wanted to "work towards a new way of allocating money within the NHS, so that hospitals treating more patients received more income. There also needed to be a closer, clearer connection between the demand for health care, its cost and the method for paying for it"[9].

Her remedies were establishing self-governance in NHS trusts and encouraging private-sector delivery of services. The mantra was that the money should follow the patient, "simulating within the NHS as many as possible of the advantages which the private sector and market choice offered, but without privatisation"[10].

John Major (1990-1997)

Thatcher's successor John Major took a more conciliatory line on public-sector reform. He was less negative about public-sector management, acknowledging that while many public services were "excellent" others could be "patronising and arrogant", run more for the "'convenience of the providers than the users"[11]. Major was not as strident as Thatcher about privatisation, believing that public-sector services could be improved while remaining in state control, but he was just as fervent about the need for reform. Consistent with his predecessor's criticism of "producer-focused" public-sector managers, he wanted providers to be more service-orientated, a shift that he believed could be encouraged by the empowerment of consumers.

Major believed targets, standards and league tables would serve as surrogates for competition, creating pressure to improve. The ideas were encapsulated in the Citizen's Charter. Major instructed all ministers to develop plans for improving service performance. He set up a unit within government — the Office of Public Service Standards — to cajole ministers and review their plans and achievements. To recognise achievements he created the Charter Mark, an award for service excellence.

Major saw independent inspection as a vital tool in the armoury of reform, reinforcing the role of the Audit Commission and introducing the Office for Standards in Education (Ofsted) to drive up standards in education.

Targets and standards were quickly adopted by the Audit Commission, magnifying its influence on public-service operations. Adherence to targets and standards were central to Audit Commission reports, evaluating the performance of councils against centrally directed criteria[12]. Likewise the Next Steps Agencies initiated under Thatcher were obliged to adopt Major's charter ideas, in his view increasing transparency and accountability.

Tony Blair (1997-2007)

Elected in 1997, New Labour's Tony Blair was more technocratic in his zeal for reform than his Conservative predecessors. He agreed with Thatcher and Major on the issue of 'producer-driven' services, arguing that 'public-sector ethos' was a cover for poor performance and that 'choice' would drive improvement. Blair labelled reform as 'modernisation', clearly signalling his belief that the public sector was behind the times and only the private sector had the know-how to bring it up to date. He felt that previous Conservative administrations had achieved little in terms of genuine reform, leaving in place inefficient monopolistic public services that were still hurting the people they were supposed to help — the poor.

Blair's mantra was 'efficiency'. He scrapped the 'compulsory' in CCT and emphasised instead that procurement should focus on 'value-for-money'[13]. Pressing forward with reform of the health service, he oversaw the establishment of 'foundation hospitals' which, like his predecessors' trusts, set out to link expenditure with performance.

Blair expanded the inspection regime, establishing the Healthcare Commission, the Commission for Social Care Inspection and Her Majesty's Inspectorate of Constabulary, and extended Ofsted's remit to cover children's services. He also expanded the Audit Commission's inspection activities in local government and extended its reach to housing associations. These activities were dovetailed with National Service Frameworks, Public Service Agreements and Local Area Agreements. In 2002 the Audit Commission started to use Comprehensive Performance Assessments, the results of which were published as league tables. In Blair's era the Audit Commission was expected to join with government in devising ways to effect real change, beginning a relationship with government that meant it was no longer independent, but more an instrument of change[14].

Under Blair, the internet was co-opted into the modernisation programme. An Electronic Service Delivery (ESD) target stipulated that one quarter of dealings with government should be digitally enabled via television, telephone or computer. To that end in 2001 the government issued detailed guidance notes ("Modern councils, modern services — access for all"[15]) that local councils were expected to follow to exploit the 'e-revolution'. Digital services promised the benefits of efficiency — cheaper transactions. The guidance, following Thatcher's and the private sector's emphasis on economies of scale, was a compendium of 'solutions' developed by the big consultancies and IT firms: access to services via call centres and digital 'channels', back offices where services would be delivered more 'seamlessly', tied together with new IT systems, essential for the programme to work. The ESD target guidance anticipated that councils would "take full advantage of the strategic opportunities available with local and private sector partners"[16].

Blair's ministers followed this agenda. For example, Home Secretary David Blunkett obliged police forces to create regional call centres and Frank Dobson as Health Secretary set up NHS Direct to deliver medical services over the phone. Deputy Prime Minister John Prescott initiated the development of regional call centres for the Fire and Rescue Service.

In 2001 Blair instituted a No 10 'Delivery Unit' with a brief to oversee and monitor performance improvement. Like Thatcher's Efficiency Unit and Major's Office of Public Service Standards the Delivery Unit's remit was to review and challenge plans for improvement, but it differed in being more programmatic and structured. Its leader, Michael Barber, later to join McKinsey, coined the term 'deliverology' to describe what he called the "science of delivery". The delivery unit sat alongside a strategy unit, set up to plan strategy and develop ideas for reform.

Blair employed Sir Peter Gershon, recruited from the private-sector, to run the Office of Government Commerce overseeing procurement across Whitehall. In 2004 his eponymous report put at £20bn the savings that could be made by improving procurement, standardising policies and procedures and simplifying, standardising and sharing support services such as HR, IT and finance in 'back offices', with these initiatives to be benchmarked across the public sector[17].

It was Gordon Brown, then Chancellor of the Exchequer, who invented the phrase "invest to save". What it meant was that local authorities could use cash from Whitehall to create call centres and back offices. Jim Murphy, minister at the Cabinet Office, claimed that sharing services would realise efficiency savings of up to 20%[18]. The wave of sharing services in central and local government began.

Blair, like his predecessors, believed in the importance of 'choice' and competition, arguing that competition was essential if choice is to work. Competition, he believed, would give producers a strong incentive to make better use of resources and drive them to devolve power to service users. Blair's administration coined the term 'double devolution' — devolution that went beyond local authorities and passed power instead to local communities.

At the end of his term of office Blair summarised his approach to public service reform as a combination of top-down pressure from government, 'choice and voice' creating pressure from citizens, competitive provision of services, and efforts to build the capability and capacity of the civil service[19].

Gordon Brown (2007-2010)

As chancellor, Gordon Brown gained a reputation for micro-managing public-sector reform. As far as he could, being soon up to his neck in the financial crisis, he continued in the same vein as prime minister.

Brown's stamp on the public-service reform agenda was to combine excellence with 'fairness'. He believed that fairness would improve social mobility. His policy pronouncement ('Excellence and Fairness', 2008) was a three-pronged model of "empowering citizens", "fostering professionalism", and "strong strategic government"[20].

Brown sought to end 'postcode lotteries' by establishing universal entitlements to basic standards. He argued that the rising aspirations of citizens required public services to be tailored to meet their individual circumstances. To that end he introduced personal budgets in care and disability services. Like Major he emphasised the need for clear, comparable information about service quality; 'user satisfaction' became a key measure of success. Echoing his predecessors, Brown wanted to put citizens in control while also unleashing a 'new professionalism' in public services[21].

Continuing Blair's pursuit of efficiencies through information technology, Brown's chancellor, Alistair Darling, sought help from Martin Read, previously CEO of the prominent IT company Logica. Contributing to Darling's Operational Efficiencies Programme, Read claimed that billions could be saved in IT expenditures and back offices[22].

Towards the end of his short tenure, Brown initiated the idea of local services pooling budgets and allocating resources according to need. This initiative was called 'Total Place'.

The coalition (2010-)

When the Conservative / Liberal Democrat coalition government took office, it looked at first as if there would be a distinctive change in philosophy. Prime Minister David Cameron vowed to end central targets — but the culture persists and targets remain alive and well in many services. His government dissolved the Audit Commission, but not the specifications and inspection culture that is the organisation's legacy.

In essence, Cameron promised more of the same but without some of the targets: more choice, more decentralisation, a more diverse range of providers, fairer access and accountability. He kept on Gershon and Read, who had previously advised the Labour government on reform, and also Lord Freud, Labour's counsellor on welfare reform.

In his first year Cameron promised to localise power, extend the use of personalised budgets for care-service users and cut the burdensome bureaucracy of regulation on front-line staff. He also vowed to increase the diversity of provision by the use of 'payment by results'. He envisaged services like health, prisons, probation and care being delivered by local authorities, voluntary or private-sector providers. Part of this diversity was articulated as the 'Big Society'. The idea was that many local needs would be better served by organisations within communities. It was followed by the Localism Act (2011) which gave new powers to communities to take over public assets and control local development. In the same year Cameron created local police and crime commissioners

Cameron continued with Brown's idea of pooling local budgets (Total Place) but re-named it 'community budgeting', giving local services investment funds to join up local services. In the same vein ministers allocated investment funding to local authorities to focus on resolving the needs of 'troubled families'. These initiatives were forecast to deliver hundreds of millions of pounds in savings.

Cameron's plans for welfare and health reform represented a continuation of a policy adopted by all previous administrations, but now with greater emphasis on private-sector involvement. The centrepiece of welfare reform was 'Universal Credit'. Designed by Iain Duncan Smith, briefly leader of the Conservative party before becoming a minister in Cameron's cabinet, its intention was to simplify the benefits and credits systems while at the same time ensuring that people were incentivised to work. Cameron's team talked of "scroungers" who, because of the welfare system, were encouraged to be dependent on state handouts[23]. Assessments for eligibility were outsourced to the private sector.

A new Efficiency and Reform Group was formed in the Cabinet Office. One of its major interventions was to extend the outsourcing of public services to private-sector providers in police services, prisons, custody management, probation for 'low risk' offenders, electronic tagging of offenders and the 'work programme' — helping people back into work. Much of this was done on the basis of 'payment by results'.

The Efficiency and Reform Group also pushed harder for shared services, echoing previous administrations' arguments for economies of scale. Central government departments were at first encouraged, then obliged, to share services and local authorities were subjected to a sustained campaign of promotion of its benefits.

Health did not escape attention. The coalition strengthened the emphasis on financial discipline for hospital and other trusts. It also extended the scope for private sector involvement by requiring services to be put out to tender to "any willing provider" and through commissioning, where the intention is to favour large-scale providers who will drive down costs.

A political consensus

Over the past 35 years there has been no real deviation in the approach to public sector reform. Whether it is via an Efficiency Unit, an Office of Public Service Standards, a Delivery Unit or an Efficiency and Reform Group, the role of the centre has been to promulgate what it thinks as worthy and pressurise the public sector to comply with its directives.

All governments have employed the idea of 'reviewing' performance, whether through meetings led by ministers or through inspection and regulation. All have believed in the supremacy of private-sector know-how and all have accepted without question the power of competition and choice. All have been wedded to the pursuit of economies of scale and IT as a means of achieving them.

If there are differences they are matters of emphasis, not philosophy — Conservative administrations, for example, placing more emphasis on outsourcing, Labour governments relying more on an apparatus of targets, specifications and inspection.

I invite you to consider this history against the numbers. The primary purpose of reform has been and still is the reduction in costs, yet costs have risen inexorably. The astute reader will be thinking that correlation is not necessarily cause and effect: quite so. So we have to look in some detail at what the reforms have meant in practice to understand how they have driven costs up.

Part 1: The industrialisation of public services

Introduction

Over the last 35 years public services have been industrialised. The underlying assumption is that bigger is better; that is, consolidating work in large centres — service factories — will yield economies of scale, i.e. lower operating costs. This is a view that has been advocated by the big consultancies and IT firms — indeed, without IT, service industrialisation would not have been possible. Private-sector organisations that followed this path have, in recent times, pulled back from the pursuit of scale as industrialisation. With the benefit of the rudder of profit, they are learning that scale in this form drives costs up and worsens service. The public sector has no rudder of profit; instead, if it has a rudder, it is a rudder of compliance.

To understand how industrialisation increases costs and worsens service we have to look at its components: call centres, back offices, shared services, outsourcing and IT systems.

Chapter 2: Call centres

Local authority call centres

I was with David Parsons in late 2010, when he was the leader of Leicestershire County Council, meeting because he held the portfolio for performance improvement on behalf of the Local Government Association. We were in his office in the council buildings. I said I was sure his council would have complied with the government target to have a call centre by 2005. He concurred. I said I bet that when it opened, it experienced more calls than had been estimated in the plan. His response was, "How did you know?"

I first saw the phenomenon in the mid-1980s when the advent of automated call distribution systems enabled the creation of call centres. In the pursuit of lower costs, private-sector companies moved telephone calls out of local branches and consolidated them in large offices in low-wage parts of the country (consultancies were making money out of maps of the UK annotated with local wage-rates). While staff costs (pay) did fall, the cost of services did not.

It was a simple error, the same trap that local authorities fell into 20 years later: treating 'telephone work' as something that could be abstracted from a service operation and processed in a stand-alone unit. As in Leicestershire, the immediate consequence is an increase in the volume of calls, because customers aren't getting what they need and have to call again to follow up. I labelled it 'failure demand' — *demand caused by a failure to do something or do something right for a customer* [1]. You might be surprised to learn that failure demand can account for as much as 80% of all demand into public services.

Note that I am not arguing against providing services over the telephone. My point is that the focus should be the design of the service — constraining the design by imposing a means of delivery is starting from the wrong end. Starting from design, you learn that some services can be provided by phone and some can't.

I explained the flaws in the rush to build local-authority call centres — learned with private-sector clients — to Howard Flight, then an opposition MP, early in 2005. Via parliamentary questions, Flight asked Phil Hope, the then (Labour) Junior Minister in the Office of the Deputy Prime Minister, for details of government directives to councils to build call centres, how much government money was being invested in them, and their cost-effectiveness[2]. Hope replied that there were no specific investments, no appraisals of cost-effectiveness and no directives. It was a politician's response, for there were, by his own admission, 'supplementary funds' provided by government and very clear directives for all local authorities to produce plans, route maps and milestones for achieving the 'ESD target' (see page 18), which included call centres.

The only unequivocal truth in Hope's answer was that there was no evaluation. Instead he asserted that local authorities recognised the contribution call centres make to effective service delivery. It's a politician's logic: we think this is a good idea, we oblige you to do it, if asked about its efficacy we can say you think it's a good idea and we judge the efficacy of the policy by the amount of compliance.

Towards the end of Labour's period in office Whitehall put out an even stronger call-centre directive to local authorities. A joint venture between the Treasury and the Local Government Association called 'Local Partnerships' developed an intervention dubbed DECATS (Delivering Efficiency, Capability and Transformational Services), provided by one of the big consultancies. Part funded by central government, DECATS included the idea that all telephone contact made by service departments would be more efficiently handled if moved to a call centre[3].

Taking telephone work out of a service and placing it in a call centre was done in the erroneous belief that it would reduce costs — in fact it just increased failure demand. The same premise is behind moving complete services to the phone.

NHS Direct

Labour secretary of state for health Frank Dobson kicked off NHS Direct in 1998 with a number of 'pilot schemes'. The idea was to staff telephone lines with trained nurses to whom those in need could have access at any time of day. Dobson argued that a telephone service would not only be "effective and popular", it would also reduce demand into other NHS services[4].

By January 1999 NHS Direct had received one-and-a-half million calls and was hailed a success. As time went on demand continued to rise. For example in the eighteen month period leading up to November 2001 call volumes to West Midlands NHS Direct rose from 16,000 a month to 30,000[5].

This was déjà vu. In the 1980s, private-sector managers had pointed to higher-than-expected call volumes as proof of the popularity of their service. Actually it should have been seen as a warning of the reverse. In just the same way, NHS Direct leaders ignored the signal of potential failure demand, boasting instead of the volume of calls handled and the speed at which they were answered.

It didn't take long for NHS Direct to earn the sobriquet 'NHS Redirect', reflecting anecdotal stories of the number of callers being referred on to Accident and Emergency departments, pharmacists and GP surgeries. What was never, and still isn't, understood is how the service works from the citizen's point of view — how often, for example, callers' problems are solved at first pass and how many calls are passed on to further transactions. If high volumes of calls to NHS Direct are merely additional transactions, overall costs can only be rising, not falling. We know from our own work in health services that failure demand is very high[6].

The only research we could find showed that NHS Direct did nothing to reduce demand on A&E services[7] and *may have* restrained increasing demand on out-of-hours GP services. The fall in the rate of growth when compared to growth in the volumes of calls, however, was trivial.

Such as it is, other evidence is mixed, to say the least. While the regulator reported that NHS Direct was "doing a good job"[8], the consumer magazine *Which?* published a report showing nurses failing to diagnose critical illness[9]. By its own account ('official' figures), two thirds of callers were referred on inappropriately[10].

By 2008 NHS Direct was costing £139m and more than £25 per call — as much as the cost of visiting a GP[11]. Calls for a proper evaluation of the service went unheeded[12]. Instead in 2010 Andrew Lansley, health secretary in the coalition government, took up the previous Labour government's plan to introduce a new number (111) that would be staffed by unqualified personnel following computer scripts. The aim was to bear down on costs: contracts — open to private-sector providers and NHS Direct — were let at a cost of £7 per call with specified 'service levels' (time to pick up the phone).

It is hardly surprising that the new 111 service providers were soon plagued by low staff morale and high turnover[13]. Imagine having someone on the other end of the phone whom you are obliged to take through time-consuming record-making procedures while they want to talk about their problem; and then you having to follow scripts that mean you will ask stupid questions instead of actually listening to what they have to say. As one user said, it seems as if the questions are designed to be delaying tactics[14]. 111 staff described themselves as in a state of panic, trying to get help for people who clearly need it.

Private-sector contractors and regional NHS Direct organisations pulled out of their contracts (some before even starting) as the contracts they were working to would be 'unsustainable' — i.e. not economically viable[15]. Other contractors drove their costs down by sacking managers ('changing the management structure'). Today the problems remain; the anecdotal evidence of failure mounts, callers are put at risk, even die, while ambulances are dispatched on unnecessary journeys[16], and we have no idea if the service achieves its purposes.

Police call centres

As Home Secretary in the Blair era, David Blunkett presided over the continued regionalisation of call centres in policing[17]. He was confident they would meet the public desire for sharp improvements in police customer service by improving access and providing callers with better information on what will happen next in their case. He also believed that centralised call-handling would lower costs. In common with other examples, no before and after comparison costs are known, however. They were never part of the plan, perhaps because no one questioned the idea that doing it this way must be cheaper. But costs can only have risen.

We have had the opportunity to study what happens in police call centres built in the Blunkett era. They correspond to a 'take-one, label it, ship it' design: every call has to be recorded and shipped on electronically to one of a multitude of police departments (each with its own specialist function) sitting behind the call centre. Many electronic records are wrongly routed, many trivial requests that could have been answered speedily take off on a labyrinthine journey; many seriously important calls get swamped as they wait in undifferentiated queues of 'work'.

In most police forces there is no awareness of these problems. Call-centre managers simply report on call volumes and service levels (how quickly they pick up the phone). The incidence, or indeed existence, of failure demand (which, as with local authorities, runs as high as 80%) is largely unknown. Yet reflecting the exact opposite of Blunkett's aspiration, failure demand is a direct measure of citizens' experience of calling the police. Blunkett thought the call centres would mean citizens would be told what would happen next. What did predictably happen next was citizens became frustrated as their issue got buried in an electronic jungle.

The extent of the damage done to police performance by accumulating failure demand is revealed when forces design a telephone service that works (see Chapter 12). The result is a dramatic liberation of capacity that was previously consumed by adherence to an apparently plausible but fundamentally wrong-headed idea.

Housing repairs

When it took on responsibility for auditing housing services, the Audit Commission encouraged the use of call centres as 'best practice'[18]. In the repairs services this meant, in short, someone who knew nothing about plumbing (the tenant) talking to someone else who knew nothing about plumbing (the call centre worker) who would choose from the Schedule of Rates (a book listing jobs and materials to be used) a job code that would determine what the plumber should do. To put it mildly, this is unlikely to be a recipe for getting it right first time. In housing services that complied with the Audit Commission's directive the level of failure demand was typically 40% or more. I will return to housing repairs.

A focus on cost

All of the problems above have, at their heart, a focus on cost. It is a paradox that will be repeated as we proceed: if you focus on cost, your costs rise.

In the drive to build call centres there have been two fundamental errors:

Assuming that telephone work is something that can be optimised in isolation from the service as a whole

Failing to study and understand the effectiveness of services provided over the phone.

The advocates of call centres assume that transaction costs are the same as the costs of providing a service. The costs of a service are end-to-end, which will include the total number of times people have to call to get the service they need.

Go and have a look.

If you're able to, go to any call centre. Put on a headset and listen to calls. Explain to the call handler you are there to understand more about why customers/citizens call. For each call ask yourself: from the caller's point of view was this call value demand (the reason the service exists) or is it the result of something we have failed to do or not done right at a previous contact?

Failure demand is a major consumer of capacity. It is, by definition, a sign of poor quality and high cost.

Chapter 3: Back Offices

When I began working in organisations in the 1970s no one used the phrase 'back office'. Such a thing did not exist. Today the back office is an unchallenged feature of organisational life, its claim to represent good practice and low cost in service delivery being taken for granted. The concept fits both the current philosophy of management and the political narrative.

One of the first pieces of work Vanguard did with local authorities was in housing benefits. In 2004 Mark Radford, the manager responsible for housing benefits at Kent's Swale Borough Council, called me to say he had read *Freedom from Command and Control* [1] and felt as though the book had been written about his own organisation. Radford's benefits service had been vilified in the local press for being the worst in the country. He had recently complied with the Department of Work and Pensions' (DWP) directive to create a back office and subsequently experienced sharp growth in the volume of work. Correctly, he understood the increase as a warning and decided to take action.

I went to visit. The DWP 'help team' had advised him to hire a private-sector 'backlog-busting' firm to help reduce the backlog. He knew it was the wrong thing to do. I learned subsequently that all housing benefits services had been obliged to follow the DWP directive with the same consequences — backlogs in the new back offices. The backlogs had created a market for private-sector backlog-busters.

The DWP initiative had been funded from Gordon Brown's 'invest to save' scheme. A total of £200m had been made available to encourage local authorities to reconfigure their housing benefits offices as separate front and back offices, tied together with IT systems to pass work to and fro. Unfortunately, such a design for housing benefits or, for that matter, any other service, can only lead to poor service and higher costs.

Like many bad management fads, the 'back office' idea originated in the US. When I teach students I impress on them the need to ask four questions every time a lecturer introduces an idea or management tool: who invented it? What problem was he or she trying to solve? Do I have that problem? And how do I know? You might be surprised to know that many lecturers, particularly those who teach 'improvement' tools like 'lean', can't answer the first two questions; some can't answer the last two, either.

So who invented the back office? Step forward Richard Chase, an American academic, who wrote an article for the *Harvard Business Review* in 1978[2] in which he argued that managers of service organisations needed to be more technocratic in their thinking.

Service managers are trained to worry about three things: how much work comes in, how many employees they have and how long the latter take to do the work (I call this the 'core paradigm' for service management and will summarise its flaws later — see Chapter 15). It follows that managers will focus their primary attention on optimising the use of their human resource, i.e. sweating the labour. This is why service centre workers are so heavily monitored.

Chase pointed out that in service organisations, the employees are frequently 'interrupted' in their tasks by customer visits or calls (wretched people!) that effectively prevent them from working at full efficiency. To solve this perceived problem, Chase proposed that a 'front office' should be employed to gather information on what customers want which could then be sent to a 'back office' where labour could now be optimised — sweated — without tiresome interference. He described this as "de-coupling the service from the customer".

These new administration factories, he postulated, should employ the concepts and language of manufacturing: batch scheduling, inventory control, work measurement and simplification. To facilitate work measurement, processes should be standardised and specialised. The argument was, and is, that this arrangement will lead to economies of scale and reduced transaction costs.

Here's how such a set-up operates in the private sector (in housing benefits it is, if anything, simpler). Front-office staff talk to the customer, as a result of which an electronic record is created which is passed to the back office, in practice often split into a number of separate functions, for each to carry out its own specialised task to meet the demand. The back-office functions work to service-level agreements (how quickly they will complete tasks), standard times (adherence to the expected time it takes to do a task) and targets for performance (amount of activity). Managers assume that the work will arrive in the right places, the workers receiving it will have the right expertise and will do the work in the standard times, and will return it within the terms of the service-level agreement. That is to say, managers think that if people just did as they should according to this logic the organisation would deliver at optimum efficiency. Pleasant dreams[3].

To shake managers from their pleasant dream, we get them to follow a customer request all the way through their system and focus on a single question: when the response was delivered, was it 'clean' (i.e. complete, not requiring the customer to call again or otherwise follow up)? It is invariably the case that the first request fails the test. Equally invariably managers rationalise the failure as an exception, because to accept it as generally true would undermine everything they have focused on as managers. So we invite them to follow another, and another...

In a very short time, what they discover is that very little goes out clean. The front-office / back-office design is a primary cause of failure demand. That's what Radford and his team learned in Swale. They found that failure demand was running at a high rate and that people claiming benefits had to present a number of times before they could get their benefit sorted; which, in turn, filled the back office with more 'tasks' for the same person.

Back offices commit the error of assuming that front- and back-office employees will have the same view of the customer. In the front office they deal with flesh-and-blood customers, in the back office what matters is adherence to rules. Two views, the difference between which can only serve to create failure demand — while back-office designs assume that rules and standardisation of work will lead to efficiency, people presenting to the front office obstinately refuse to come in standard sizes. Service demand is inherently varied — 'customers' are not all the same.

As Radford and his housing benefits team were the first to learn, the context within which people make claims for benefits — what's going on in their lives — far from being irrelevant is vitally important for developing a service that works, that is, that solves their problem and stops them coming back repeatedly. So the Swale team abandoned the back office and replaced it with a face-to-face service, following the steps I shall outline in Part 2. Like others who followed them they achieved profound results: it took them from being one of the worst in the country to one of the best, in a matter of months.

Back offices serve to ensure that context is not taken into account; standardising processes ensures that they are insensitive to customer needs. 'De-coupling' a customer from a service is a sure way to stop the service working. It is the last thing a service manager would want to do.

Chase's proposition is based on the same mistaken assumption as call centres: that transaction costs are identical to the cost of service. The reality is that while transaction costs may fall, the total cost of service rises. We go back to our mantra: if we manage by focusing on cost, we drive costs up.

We should abandon the idea of front and back offices; they have no contribution to make to effective service design.

Go and have a look.

If you can, go to where work arrives in any back office.
Follow the steps I outlined above to shake the pleasant dream.

I have described the problems present in any back-office design. These days the term 'back office' is often used to describe the centralisation and sharing of support functions such as HR, finance, legal and administration. In these examples, creating a back office means moving common departments to a central service. While their designs exhibit the same problematic as Chase's notion of the back office, their purpose is not only to sweat the labour, it is to achieve wider economic benefit from 'economies of scale'. We shall go there next.

Chapter 4: Shared services –
Are there economies of scale?

In September 2010 I shared a platform at a Conservative party conference fringe event with Bob Neill, then a minister at the Department for Communities and Local Government. We were discussing sharing services. Neill said that if, for example, there were six fire and rescue services in an area and they all had back offices doing things like personnel and finance, then it was 'obvious' that sharing these services would lead to lower costs. I asked how this would lead to less work being done. He didn't answer.

Perhaps it was an unfair question, for I knew that Neill would be thinking about the savings made by having fewer managers, fewer buildings and, more speculatively, only one IT system. These are 'less-of-a-common-resource' savings, which are real and unequivocal, if not always easy to realise. While it isn't too difficult to sack managers there is usually a one-off cost in redundancy payments — you might also wonder why, if services can run with fewer managers, that knowledge hasn't been acted on already. Building savings can only be realised if the premises surplus to requirements are sold or the costs of maintaining them passed to another organisation. Existing IT contracts often have to be unwound, at not insignificant cost. Sometimes the claimed IT savings are based on the fact that (say) six IT systems have been replaced by buying one new one. This is like claiming you made savings at the sales when actually you spent money.

But these less-of-a-common-resource savings are never the big numbers in business cases for sharing services. The big savings always relate to lower transaction costs. The notion is that the greater the volume of work being put through the system, the lower the transaction costs. This may be true as far as it goes, but it is irrelevant, another example of the 'sales' fallacy: doing something cheaply isn't a saving if it shouldn't need to be done in the first place, and it is even worse — a monstrous perpetual motion machine — if doing it creates yet more work to be done. We need to face up to it: economy of scale is a myth[1]. I knew something Neill didn't: that creating a back office (whether sharing it or not) will increase the work to be done, not lessen it.

We have seen how a focus on transaction costs drives costs up in call centres and back offices; by sharing services we simply ratchet up the problem by taking it to a higher level. That is the Achilles heel of shared services, and it is insidious.

Here's how a shared-service project usually plays out. The business plan promises modest less-of-a-common-resource savings and large transaction-cost savings. It includes a large investment in new IT systems and 'transformation' activities. Set-up costs are put against the long-term savings, so major savings are only scheduled to accrue in the later stages of the plan. In the short term the less-of-a-common-resource savings are duly realised, building confidence that the venture is on plan. IT problems are frequent, sometimes resulting in complete project failure (see Chapter 6). But even if those are overcome, over time costs begin to rise. Hapless public-sector leaders charged with delivering the plan remain persuaded by their consultancy 'partners' that things will get better (after all they share a common faith in the eventual achievement of economies of scale) and they put a positive spin on things. When the chickens come home to roost and realisation finally dawns that there are no long-term savings to be had, there is one final shock in store: getting out of the venture, particularly if it is a 'partnership' with a private-sector provider, will cost millions more. Sometimes the exit costs are so high that the only option is to stay with what is now a costly and poor-quality service.

It is not as though we are short of evidence on the failures of sharing services. In 2012 the National Audit Office published a review of shared-service initiatives in five government departments or agencies, viz the Department for Environment, Food and Rural Affairs, the Department for Transport (DfT), DWP, the Ministry of Justice, and Research Councils

UK[2]. The business plans estimated a total implementation cost of £900m for the five ventures, to deliver joint savings of £159m by the end of 2010-11. In the event, by 2012 the cost had risen to £1.4bn, and not one made a saving. One venture was reported to have broken even, while the two others that bothered to track benefits reported the reverse, losses of £255m. Note that not all ventures tracked results. And when they did, they measured them against the plan, not the cost of services before they were shared.

The failure to establish base-line service costs, and thus a yardstick against which results could be judged, is a measure of unquestioning official faith that economies will follow from the venture. Sir Peter Gershon had assured both Labour and Coalition ministers that there was massive scope for improvement through sharing services[3]. Their confidence was bolstered by the finding of his report that similar projects had produced important savings in both the private and public sectors. In fact, Gershon's private-sector evidence was taken from an earlier study by Martin Read[4], whose sources in turn were the big consultancies which, to say the least, are hardly disinterested observers in the matter of shared services. Gershon's public-sector cases included the DfT venture which was subsequently described by the Public Accounts Committee as displaying "stupendous incompetence", with costs rising from £55m to £121m, in the process wiping out any savings[5], and Southwest One, which was later to fail spectacularly (see below).

Working primarily in the private sector, I am familiar with many examples of comprehensive shared-service failure, but not surprisingly they are rarely acknowledged in public. They fall over for the reasons discussed here: poorly designed and implemented IT projects and high levels of failure demand caused by industrial designs.

UK Research Councils

One of the cases reported on by the NAO was the shared-services venture for the seven UK Research Councils. In January 2006 the responsible Department (the then Department of Trade and Industry) instructed the councils to centralise and share back-office functions comprising HR services, IT support, invoice processing, expense claims and the administration of grants, with 'full harmonisation' to be achieved by 2009. The plan was to realise efficiency savings within the next spending period (2008-09 to 2010-11), with total savings for the first 10 years of operation forecast to hit £395 million.

Problems started early on as efficiency-savings targets were missed[6]. In 2010, David Delpy, chief executive of the new operation, remained confident that over the period the planned savings would be achieved[7]. But others were having doubts. Writing in the Science and Technology Facilities Council's annual report for 2011-12, chief executive John Womersley reported that service levels at the centre were "significantly below expected standards"[8]. Other research councils highlighted continuing problems with payments and risks with IT application security[9]. It cost £13m to terminate a contract with the IT supplier involved, and in 2012 the NAO report said the venture was showing a net cost of £126m.

Meanwhile, users were reduced to blogging — their only outlet — complaints that grant administration had slowed to a crawl and the quality of service was at best patchy[10]. The complaints were typical of people's frustration with trying to get services from industrialised designs, which are built to deliver the packages the producer has decided on, not to respond positively to customer need. Users do, however, report being 'discouraged' from talking negatively about their experiences of the new regime.

Account NI

Account NI is a shared-service centre set up to process financial transactions for Northern Ireland's government departments. It originated in 2000 when a review estimated that a scheme could be operational by 2003 at a cost of £63m. As the project developed, timescales and costs rose. By 2006 the delivery date had slipped to 2009 while the cost had mounted to £169m. In 2011 the total project cost was declared to be £187m. The National Audit Office for Northern Ireland identified a further £26m in costs that should have been included, taking the total cost to £213m[11].

In 2014 the Northern Ireland Assembly Public Accounts Committee described the cost of paying invoices through the shared service as 'extraordinarily high' at almost £10 per payment, and complained that there was no clear evidence that the new service had delivered value for money[12].

Investigations revealed that client departments were employing extra people to cope with invoicing and payment problems, making a planned staff reduction of £43m impossible to achieve[13]. (Reflect on this: a £213m investment to deliver a £43m saving.)

Arguments rumble on. The Auditor General is critical of the failure to monitor developments, while the Permanent Secretary of the Department of Finance claims Account NI to be "a success story"[14], and the Finance Minister, who disputes the findings of the audit office and accounts committee, says Northern Ireland's shared services are "an exemplar not just in Europe but in the world" which has "caught the interest of other governments"[15].

Southwest One

Southwest One (SW 1) was a joint shared-service venture between Somerset County Council, Taunton Deane Borough Council, Avon and Somerset Police, and IBM. It began in 2007 with the usual promises of efficiency savings. Like many other ventures it had problems with the IT component[16] and by 2011 it was reporting a loss over the first three years of operation[17]. In the same year Somerset County Council renegotiated the contract in order to take most of the services back in-house, which in the words of the local MP left SW 1 as "little more than an IT supplier"[18].

In February 2012 the Conservative leader of Somerset County Council launched a blistering attack on SW 1, describing it as "failing" and delivering "staggering" losses[19]. Even worse news was that the council felt it could not walk away from the contract because the cost of doing so was prohibitive: it had no option but to stick with it[20]. On top of that there have been multi-million pound contract disputes and millions spent in settlements[21].

By now readers will be getting the picture. These examples are broadly typical of what happens in any shared-service venture.

I should add that before the launch of the NAO report, towards the end of 2011, I attended a discussion at which the high-level results were presented along with the Office's conclusions on the failures of shared services. I made the points discussed here, but nothing of what I had to say appeared in the final report. Most of the other attendees were from IT companies providing shared-services platforms. To say I was not popular is an understatement.

Unperturbed by the burgeoning evidence, in 2012 Francis Maude, minister for the Cabinet Office, published a business case called *'Next generation back-office shared services for Government'*[22] which looked to "extend shared services beyond the back office to the front office" — in other words, call centres should be subject to the same centralisation and sharing as back offices. The plan is for an 'independent' shared-services facility, a euphemism for a joint venture with the private sector. According to Cabinet Office estimates, the new centre would require "an investment of between £44 million and £95 million" and save between £67 million and £128 million a year at a minimum. Within these numbers is a 'saving' described as avoiding software upgrade costs, which looks a bit like desperation[23].

It is at first sight surprising that Amyas Morse, the head of the NAO, endorsed the Cabinet Office business case. Tellingly, he resolved the dissonance by accepting the government line that it had been a mistake to make sharing services voluntary and allow services to be tailored to the needs of different departments. If departments were compelled to share and to work with standardised processes, Morse reasoned, shared services would deliver their promise[24].

Nothing could illustrate more clearly the strength of the ideological belief in scale, and the refusal to accept the possibility that there might be an alternative. Yet in practical fact, Morse couldn't be more wrong. Standardising a service prevents it from dealing with the variety of demand, so the costs of shared services can only rise along with failure demand and the blood pressure of frustrated 'customers'.

As in central, so also in local government, where a veritable campaign in favour of shared services has been raging, orchestrated by Whitehall, the Local Government Association (LGA), and, of course, private-sector providers (often through the think tanks they sponsor). The LGA now boasts of 337 local authorities operating 383 shared-services initiatives[25]. However, the good news, if you can call it that, is that the bulk of these initiatives are in-house ventures that have merely achieved less-of-a-common-resource savings, which can be deduced from the numbers: the claimed savings amount to only £357m, less than £1m per initiative.

We can also deduce that the scope for significant improvement in local-authority services remains enormous; services that are popular choices for sharing, like IT and HR, show massive potential for improvement. IT help desks, for example, typically don't help, whether shared or not. When studied and redesigned (more about this in Part 2) they do — help and do so at much lower costs.

Spurious claims

A trawl of the policy documents claiming benefits from shared services — documents provided to ministers — reveals that they often include savings reported from other ventures around the world as 'delivered' although they were merely business-case projections. Gershon fell for this in a big way, taking promised savings from public-sector ventures as delivered and accepting examples from the big consultancies' that were almost all anonymised. IT companies take advantage of gullible civil servants who, in their defence, are obliged to find 'evidence' that fits their ministers' narrative. The most glaring example among many may be the shared-services venture in Western Australia, which, in Aussie-speak, 'blew out' at a cost of $370m[26], but whose projected savings were included as 'delivered' in reports to politicians extolling the virtue of sharing services.

We have already noted that plans and promises rarely include evidence of service costs before the sharing venture, while 'savings' reports often ignore the investment costs. Finally, what is never understood is the total costs of service, the figures relying instead on 'improvements' (reductions) in transaction costs.

Despite all the evidence, the appetite for sharing services is undiminished. Ministers think with greater coercion and better project management they will succeed. They are engaged in a classic case of trying to do the wrong thing righter. I shall return to the problems of 'project management' in Chapter 6.

Yet all is not lost. In the end what matters is not where a service is located, shared or not, but how it is designed. Re-designing the services provided by shared ventures is feasible and experience shows that the result can be high-quality services capable of meeting the needs of disparate users. I shall return to the principles for better design in Part 2.

When shared services have been outsourced, however, a further difficulty presents. To this matter we turn in the next chapter.

Chapter 5: Outsourcing

At the time of Gordon Brown's inadvertent creation of a market for private-sector backlog-busters in housing benefits, we were engaged by a local authority to help it improve its housing-benefits service. It transpired that the benefits staff actually belonged to a private-sector 'partner'; not immediately obvious as agents worked in the council offices and to all intents and purposes behaved as part of the council. The results impressed council leaders. It was, they said, the kind of innovation they'd hoped for by outsourcing their services to the private-sector partner.

This led to a meeting with the chief executive of the outsource company. He too was impressed by what the housing benefits people had achieved, and excited at the revenue potential from doing the same for other councils. We were in one of the company's offices in the North East. Outside our meeting room there were groups of people working as backlog-busters for a number of local authorities. I suggested those would be a good place to start, for the firm already had a relationship with these authorities and if it followed the same method the local councils would no longer need the backlog-busting service. In my view, a great value-creating pitch. His reply was, "That's not very commercial, John".

In 2013 I was at a lunch in the City with leaders of private-sector providers of public services. One, a chief executive of a firm supplying custody management for the police, thought, as I was to him an 'improvement' man, that I'd appreciate his tale of what his firm had been doing to improve custody management. In short, he told me it had cut the time police officers are tied up with the custody-management process, releasing police officers to spend time on their 'proper' job.

I pointed out that when you study offenders going through custody suites you learn that a significant proportion of them shouldn't be going into custody at all. They will indeed have committed an offence, but for many reasons (the next step in the criminal justice system isn't ready, or they will be spared custody because of their circumstances) locking them up serves no purpose, since they will soon be released. Genuine improvement would focus on reducing the volume of work in the custody suite, a much more powerful improvement lever. The chief executive changed the subject. His firm's contract was based on volume, so the more people that go through custody suites, the more it earns.

Payment for volume of activity is a common and fundamental error in outsourcing contracts. It incentivises increased activity, the last thing that is wanted in any service, least of all one that consumes public funds. It doesn't take a genius to work out that under a volume-based contract, the more failure demand the system generates, the better it is for the outsource provider. The worse the service from the customer's point of view, the greater the benefit to the provider's revenues.

We can see this pattern in many local-authority outsourcing arrangements. Take, for example, 'Service Birmingham', essentially an outsourced call-centre and IT-support arrangement. The good news at least is that local councillors woke up to the fact that they are paying their 'partner' for servicing failure demand; but an internal inquiry blamed council departments for 'letting down' citizens[1]. They failed to understand that the causes of failure are systemic, the separation of front- and back-offices. Birmingham council has taken its call centre back in house which of itself won't solve the problem and councillors are reported to be saying that exiting the deal would be too costly[2].

Abandoning outsourcing deals is always costly. Bedford council paid £7.7m[3], Somerset £5.9m[4]. Many are kept secret for reasons of 'commercial confidentiality'. The truth of way out-of-whack costs being too embarrassing to admit, local politicians tend to put a gloss on the reasons for termination, citing for instance 'benefits from the partnership' that the council is 'now taking forward' — which is partly why such lapsed deals fail to make the national press. Nevertheless, for those who care to look, the high level of terminations is clearly telling us something important.

Francis Maude, minister for the Cabinet Office, continues to maintain that outsourcing is essential for improving public services. It is, he asserts, "in our interests". Maude believes outsourcing public-sector work to overseas facilities ('offshoring') is essential if the UK is to remain competitive, otherwise jobs will be lost in the UK[5].

Offshoring takes the idea of moving work to low-wage areas and internationalises it, still in the vain expectation that lower-cost transactions will lead to lower-cost services. Wherever they are located, they don't. Maude, like others before him, is repeating what he was told by Peter Gershon. Gershon's analysis was based on 'evidence' provided by the big consultancies, some of which have their own overseas call centres and back offices and all of which chant the mantra that service costs are identical to transaction costs. They claim that sharing services yields efficiency gains of 20-30%, outsourcing a further 10-30%, and offshoring the same again. In other words, by sharing services and outsourcing them to lower-cost operations overseas, companies can reduce costs by up to 50%[6]. This — pardon the expression — is pure horse shit. The truth is that while large and sustainable gains are achievable by improving the design of a service, sharing services without redesigning them can only release minimal less-of-a-common-resource gains. Outsourcing such unimproved services on the usual transaction-cost basis simply locks in the high costs and, from there, costs will only grow.

Since Gershon, many private-sector companies have discovered that offshoring raises costs rather than reducing them, and have consequently brought work back home (they call it, naturally, 'onshoring'!). Private-sector clients with outsourced operations — which are invariably on transaction-volume-based contracts — find that working with the 'partner' to improve service design inevitably involves new 'works orders' which attract large fees. In time they learn that the only way of achieving a fundamental redesign of the service is to take it back in-house.

Maude clearly believes that the private-sector is 'better'. It makes you wonder why companies with terrible reputations for customer service — some of which are the butt of jokes in national media — even get a look in.

None of this is to argue against outsourcing as such. Vanguard helps private-sector business-to-business services work as one system, where the books are open and gains to the provider follow gains to the whole system. And it is true that the private sector has taken the lead in developing more constructive outsourcing approaches — approaches that abandon strict contract rules and instead draw up agreements that treat the supplier as part of the same service system, working together for the same purpose.

With such an approach suppliers of custody services, for example, would, like their host police force, be focused on the end-to-end process; only in that way can both parties improve the system. Similarly with outsourcing of customer services in local authorities, cutting failure demand has to involve both parties working together on the services end-to-end; as failure demand falls everyone wins.

A feature of many outsourced service contracts is the big deal they make of providing 'new' IT systems. In practice the IT is of course not 'new' to the provider, being a re-hash of an existing system, but the fees (as ever) to the customer are large. When implementation runs into problems, as it frequently does, the cost of finding solutions too is charged to the customer; another predictable way to increase the supplier's revenues. We will look at these issues in the next chapter.

Chapter 6: Information Technology

In their aptly-entitled book *Dangerous Enthusiasms*[1], Robin Gauld and Shaun Goldfinch paint a shocking picture. Thirty per cent of large-scale IT projects fail outright and a further 60% require more time, resource and effort and/or still fail to work properly. That doesn't leave many successes. In 1995 the University of Sheffield published a report which came to much the same conclusions[2].

The IT industry is of course fully aware of these figures, but they are not something that it likes to talk about. Instead, as technology develops, the IT industry reinvents itself, each advance being promoted as *the* new means to a better future, deflecting any focus on either acknowledging past failure or understanding the reasons. Thirty years ago the 'solution' was personal computing; today it is the cloud, 'big data' and social media. The 'solutions' always involve more IT rather than less. But, as I shall argue in Chapter 11, less is better.

Public-sector IT failure

The public sector has seen its fair share of complete failures — those (the 30%) that have to be abandoned. The most expensive and well known, once described as the RMS Titanic of IT disasters, was the NHS National Programme for IT (NPfIT), which may have consumed up to £20bn — no one knows exactly — by the time it was shelved by the coalition in 2011. When the idea of a patient record was first promoted by then Prime Minister Blair, he argued that if someone from Birmingham fell ill in Blackpool, the existence of a patient record would ensure they were treated effectively. Nobody, it seemed, asked the obvious question: how many people fell over in a place where they didn't live and the lack of a record led to errors in their treatment? I have asked that question of ambulance drivers. They think long and hard before invariably answering that they can't think of one. We cannot conclude that it never happens, nor that it could never happen. But before we spend vast resources on solving a 'problem', we ought to find out whether it does happen, how often, how predictably, and with what particular deficits in information. In other words, we ought to know if there is a problem, and if there is how big it is.

I had the opportunity to speak to Jeremy Hunt, the current Health Secretary, when he launched his current initiatives for health reform. I explained that Vanguard had been studying the health system and found that much of the demand was failure demand. The primary cause of failure demand was the fragmentation of services — they were functionally designed, not patient-centric — and the way to eliminate it was to design services around people. He replied that he agreed with my analysis but not the conclusion. In his view the patient record would be the vehicle for joining up services.

To say NPfIT was shelved is not entirely accurate. Hunt is maintaining the drive for patient records, one of NPfIT's key components, but shifting responsibility for implementation to NHS trusts. In 2013 it was revealed that the NHS is still set to spend £600m on a "hopeless" patient record system supplied by a "rotten company", in the words of the chair of the Public Accounts Committee[3]. NHS Trusts that choose the anointed IT system will receive central funding; those that don't will have to purchase something else with their own money.

One of the reasons for this absurdity is the cost of unwinding the contract. After the NHS had to pay £103m to renegotiate the original deal and pay the supplier's legal costs, the civil servant responsible concluded it was not worth running the risk of encountering further legal disputes[4]. Now that the trusts have taken over responsibility, if and when the initiatives fail, they will shoulder the blame.

Fire and Rescue services

In 2004, when John Prescott was Deputy Prime Minister, he decided that the Fire and Rescue Service (FRS) would be better (i.e. more cheaply) served by regional control centres. The plan was to consolidate 46 local control rooms into nine regional centres using a national computer system. In 2010 the project was declared a complete failure, having wasted "at least £482m of taxpayers' money"[5] on IT systems that were beset with repeated problems.

Now, years after the project was cancelled, Whitehall still hasn't decided what to do with many of the specially built, high-specification facilities that are its legacy. Some remain empty. I was taken to one by an FRS officer, a gleaming new high-security facility costing millions just to keep heated. Under then chair Dr Phyllis Starkey, the parliamentary Communities and Local Government Committee published a series of thorough reports on the failure which, clearly, went unheeded[6].

As with Hunt at health, the faith of the Department for Communities and Local Government (DCLG) in regional call centres for Fire and Rescue Services remains undimmed. Again taking a leaf from Hunt's book, it has passed the responsibility for creating locally-led projects to local Fire and Rescue Services, stumping up a further £82m to fund them. It didn't take long for reports to surface of delays and revisions to the anticipated savings (downwards, in case you had any doubts).[7]

These examples are merely the tip of the iceberg of IT failure in the public sector. Dexter Whitfield produced a list which, consistent with Gauld and Goldfinch, rated about 30% of projects as complete write-offs. It is a long list![8]

Whitfield also provides damning evidence of many partial failures (the 60%).

Single Farm Payments

To take one example, the IT system for paying farm subsidies under the EU's Single Farm Payment system worked so poorly that the UK was eventually fined £327m for the failure. This was on top of IT costs that had rocketed from an original estimate of £58m to £350m, and a total of £300m spent on temporary staff by the Rural Payments Agency (RPA) to bring down the resulting backlog. Incredibly, the RPA re-hired the same consulting firm that had overseen the meltdown. It's a peculiar feature of the IT industry that failing to create value for a customer generates more revenue!

To put this in perspective, the price of the IT debacle was around five times the RPA's £169m annual running costs[9]. The RPA pays subsidies to 106,000 farmers. As Austin Mitchell, MP, a member of the Public Accounts Committee, observed, it would have been cheaper to send a member of staff around in a Rolls Royce with a bag of gold[10].

Doing the wrong thing righter

Any minister or public-sector leader of sound mind who is investing hopes in a new IT project should ask themselves why the project they are so enthusiastic about should be an exception to the majority rule — that is, actually work.

Is better project management the answer?

The first plausible idea they will be presented with is that failure of IT projects is a project management problem. Francis Maude, coalition minister for the Cabinet Office, duly set up the Project Management Academy to teach better project management and the Major Projects Authority to monitor and keep up to scratch the management of important specific projects.

The notion that project management is the problem is plausible. Some of the projects have been shambolic, and reports on them — many, of course, drawn up by the IT consultancies — have drawn attention to the need for better 'governance'.

Whitehall promotes a project-management methodology called 'Prince 2'. Many public-service managers have been through Prince-2 training. Prince 2 began life in the 1970s with the expressed goal of improving the delivery of large-scale IT systems through better project management. It was a major initiative to stem the tide of IT failure, already evident all those years ago. Ask yourself this: have we seen improvements in IT delivery and/or a reduction in IT failures over the last 30 years? Yet Prince 2 remains 'best practice'. "Surely", people say, "it must be a project management problem". The fact is that we have been trying to solve the problem with better project management for 40 years and results have obstinately refused to get better. When the only answer to repeated failure is to do the same thing again, only better, it is a sure sign that the initial premise was wrong and we are engaged in a project that no amount of better management will make come out right: doing the wrong thing righter[11].

Will Agile do it?

Iain Duncan Smith at DWP believes that the IT system at the heart of Universal Credit, his ambitious scheme for reforming benefits, will work because the IT folk are practising 'Agile'. Agile is an example of the

IT industry re-inventing itself. The idea is that IT development should reject the 'waterfall' methods conventionally employed (specify, make, implement) and instead build small-scale developments in a series of iterations where the work is done. But if the way work is done is central to the problem (as is the thesis of this book), Agile can only amount to doing the wrong thing faster.

The UC IT project is a train crash in slow motion. Because of IT problems Duncan Smith slowed the project down, saying he didn't want the whole scheme to buckle under pressure. Originally the plan was to have 4.5 million people on Universal Credit by 2015. This number has now been downgraded to 400,000[12]. The plans for UC have been re-scheduled a number of times, and the players are changed with alarming frequency[13].

I wrote to Duncan Smith in the early days of the UC initiative. In essence I explained that he faced two hurdles. The first was getting the IT system to work. But even if he got over that, it wouldn't help him with the second, which is dealing with the variety of demand. People need help with benefits and credits for complex and infinitely varied reasons. Computers have to work to rules and categories, which makes them notoriously ill-equipped to deal with variety, the first manifestation of which is high levels of failure demand into call centres.

Duncan Smith sent me to see the civil servants who were running the UC project at the time. I explained the hurdles to them and introduced them to private-sector clients who explained the expensive mistakes they had made in thinking that they could overcome the second hurdle by computer.

I even offered the DWP project team an insurance policy: we would create a face-to-face UC service in a local authority, one that had already used our method to improve a benefits service; important because it would know the principles to work with (more on these in Part 2). Compared to the UC project, which was set to cost hundreds of millions and take seven years, such a scheme could have been up and running in months and would have been a powerful test of the principle of UC: what does it take to ensure that people are able to live a normal life rather than be dependent on benefits? I express it that way because the way Duncan Smith and other ministers tell it (how do we ensure people are incentivised to work rather than claim benefits) is not a fair reflection of reality. It fits with the government's narrative of benefits users as 'strivers and skivers' (or 'scroungers'). But study on the ground shows that scroungers who need to be incentivised are few compared the number of people wanting above all to be helped to live a normal — in their terms — life. I shall return to this in Chapter 10.

None of this changed anything. UC was the government's flagship programme for 'digital by default' and it was the civil servants' job to deliver it as planned. What the civil servants did do was seek to contract with a provider to handle failure demand should UC fail in the way I predicted. I'm sure their motivation was simply to avoid bad news.

At the time of writing UC has been evaluated as being "reset" by the Major Projects Authority. This means that three years in it now has to be judged as an entirely new project.[14] Oh, and of the two civil servants I saw — one has retired, the other has been sacked.

The current efforts to improve IT development are classic examples of trying to do the wrong thing righter — a straightforward symptom of failure to understand the underlying problem.

There are two reasons for the failure of IT: the way we make it and what we make.

The way we make IT

IT development begins with a specification for what the system will provide, agreed with the client. The specification is broken up into an abundance of tasks to be completed by discrete specialist groups that need to be conscious of their works' interdependencies. Above this complex organisation sit various levels of project management and control ('governance'). Often there are more people employed in governance and progress-chasing than carrying out the work. Governance is dominated by an ethos of working to budgets and plans. So IT developers worry about meeting the budget and plan, rather than whether the IT works.

The way we make IT leads inevitably to the failures evidenced by Gauld and Goldfinch. The IT industry has become industrialised and massively complicated. The big IT companies have a vested interest in it staying that way. The number of people involved in IT development is staggering.

These industrial designs, as with the industrial designs of public services, just don't work. When failure occurs, as it always does, the response is to increase control with 'war rooms', multiplying 'reviews' and the like. Far from solving the problem, this just exacerbates it[15].

What we make

IT is the enabler of today's industrial service designs. For example, a computer 'workflow' system is needed to move information between the front and back office. Workflow is actually a misnomer. The fragmentation (specialisation) and standardisation of work and activity management that it entails amplifies work and builds inventory and thus impedes the flow of work, making the whole system less able to respond to customers. When we help service organisations redesign their service to work better for the customer, back offices disappear, and so do the associated workflow systems.

Or take local authorities' expensively acquired Customer Relationship Management (CRM) systems. Again, these are usually full of failure demand and progress-chasing. Effective services make CRM systems redundant. Like CRM and workflow systems, 'productivity management' systems to control works tradesmen also do the opposite of what they say on the tin. Like them, when the service works, they go too. And so we have a third kind of IT failure: IT that 'works' but is counterproductive and later has to be scrapped.

When private-sector companies 'get' this and grasp the scope for improvement, they abandon their workflow systems and the industrialised service designs that go with them. Unfortunately, the public sector, not having the rudder of profit, can't act so easily to undo its mistakes. Even where such arrangements are not locked in by outsourcing or shared-services contracts, the political pressure from Whitehall and regulators and 'best practice' seminars make behaving rationally difficult.

To take an example, many benefit services now deploy software that purports to be able to detect fraud over the telephone. Its protagonists argue that such a step became necessary when face-to-face service was replaced by electronic and telephone contact as part of the industrialisation of benefit services. The evidence shows these systems are poor at detecting fraud. One researcher concluded that the output generated by the software is "closer to astrology than science"[16]. He added that he was surprised it was still being used because of the "very good work done by the DWP in the UK showing it did not work".

The reaction to this evidence is instructive. Peter Fleming, a councillor who chairs the Local Government Association's improvement board, said the software was used "as part of a wider range of methods to identify cases which may need closer scrutiny". The private-sector supplier argued that the "technology is a useful additional tool in the validation process of identifying potentially fraudulent claims"[17]. In other words, when protagonists are confronted with evidence showing we are wasting money and failing to achieve the purpose, they simply deny it.

The best way to detect fraud is by meeting and talking to claimants directly — a face-to-face service. But that would fly in the face of the political narrative. Industrial designs make fraud easier — a computer is far easier to fool than a human being. Yet, however ineffective, fraud-detection software will not disappear until the industrial design itself is abandoned; just to dump it is too politically dangerous.

Abandoning IT-led change

The coalition government promised an end to large-scale IT projects[18]. But the temptation is evidently still too great. Ministers clearly believe the IT companies' propaganda about IT as a means to efficiency, even though the evidence contradicts the claim. This is not to deny that IT can do things quickly and efficiently — the problems come when IT is used for automating things that people do better (e.g. making judgements in complex circumstances), and even more so when it is treated as the enabler, the means of change.

IT is the servant not the master of service redesign — the last change element to be put in place, not the first. Change that begins with studying and redesigning service will make far more economical but much more effective use of IT, because it is based on knowledge. I shall return to this in Chapter 11. Before that we have to turn to the issue of how to design services that work.

Part 2: Delivering services that work

Introduction

Over the last ten years we have published many examples of profound improvement in public services. They show how better results are achieved by changing the system, 'the way the work works'. A change in the system requires a change in philosophy, a change in management thinking. This is a difficult thing to achieve — you can imagine how most managers react if they are told that the way they manage, everything they believe about management, is just plain wrong or, to be more accurate, suboptimal. That is the first and hardest hurdle — understanding how our current conventions in managing organisations are not only incapable of solving the problems we face but are also, unfortunately, the *cause* of many of them.

We, mankind, invented management, so we can also decide to do it differently. The evidence shows that we can make enormous strides in improving public services and reducing their costs (by a surprising amount) if we approach the problem with a different logic from conventional management thought. It is a shift from managing the parts to managing the whole, and managing the whole requires completely different thinking about the purposes and activities of management. This is not a refinement or addition to the way we currently manage — it is to renounce management 'as is' and replace it with a different philosophy and practice.

To deliver services that work it is necessary to turn the assumptions of industrialisation on their head. The uncomfortable truth — uncomfortable at least for politicians and the big consultancies that are the champions of industrialisation — is that greater economic improvement comes from flow rather than scale. Managers who have learned to manage flow cross a Rubicon. They cannot "go back" to the way they managed before. They describe the change as "liberating", a "different state of mind", a "new profession of management" — but of greatest importance is their testimony to the fact that it works![1]

In this part of the book, I shall describe the better philosophy and the means for achieving it, and give examples that show what it looks like in practice.

Chapter 7: A better philosophy

The secret of good service is to give customers what they need. Conventional management thinking would have it that notwithstanding the official rhetoric ('customer delight', 'the customer is king', etc.) this is actually impossible because it can only lead to higher costs. You will often hear managers talk about the need to 'balance' quality and cost, on the assumption that any improvement in quality will consume greater resources and raise cost. This is wrong. There is no trade-off. The counterintuitive truth is that as quality improves, costs fall.

Consider first what you learn from observing industrialised services. They fail to meet customer needs and they have high costs. The second is the direct consequence of the first, the most obvious signal being the presence of large amounts of failure demand as customers return to complain or to get the uncompleted service finished. The costs of failure demand and the increased activity it involves (absorbing expensive capacity) are the knowable costs of poor service. But the costs of customer dissatisfaction and, in the case of public services, the damage to the lives of people, families and communities, are much greater and they are unknowable.

Politicians often assert that 'customer expectations are rising', in effect implying that people are themselves to blame for unsatisfiable needs. I see no evidence of this. A more accurate interpretation of the evidence would be that customer dissatisfaction is rising and people are more inclined to complain; to receive a service that works is something beyond the norm, something unusual in this day and age.

We have seen how services that are designed to manage cost fail to give customers what they need — and thus raise cost. Now turn it round. Suppose you can design a service that gives a customer just what he or she needs and only that — what do you think will happen to costs? The secret of good service is to design against demand: that is to say, to understand customer demand(s) and create a service that meets it; in that way, costs fall.

I remember explaining to Peter Day on his BBC Radio 4 'In Business' programme[1] that managers of service organisations know little or nothing about demand in customers' terms — what their customers want from them. Day was astonished that so basic a requirement for running a service organisation should be lacking. Managers usually *think* they know about demand, having as they do proxies for understanding it (such as work volumes in types of queues). But in practice the only real thing they pay attention to is demand volume. This means that they treat all demand as 'work to be done', effectively ignoring, as I explained earlier, the potent signal of failure demand.

Understanding demand is the first key to managing flow. The way to conceptualise good service is as a design that enables customers to 'pull value' from it, something that is clearly impossible without an understanding of what demand means in customer terms.

Designing a service in this way is to (re)conceptualise our organisations as working 'outside-in' (for the customer) rather than top-down (to satisfy the management). And that is not just a slogan — it involves abandoning all the props of top-down management, such as targets, standards and budgets. Managers react to this idea badly, thinking it means 'letting go' and giving up control. This is one of the reasons why change starts with 'study' (the subject of the next chapter), for managers need to see for themselves how their current means of control are, in truth, sending their organisations out of control.

Better and productive control is achieved through the use of (different) measures at the point where the work is done that enable those who do it to understand and improve their method. This is not, as managers often think, a question of 'empowering' people; empowerment is a 'command-and-control' phrase ('*I* empower *you*'). It is, rather, to change the thinking about control so as to place it where it needs to be if we are to be successful.

Of equal importance is to equip the front line with the expertise to handle customer demands. The need is to 'smarten up' the front line, the opposite of the current emphasis on 'dumbing down'. The apparent attraction of dumbing down, of course, lies in the belief that it will reduce costs, the natural companion to the belief that smartening up will increase costs. As we have seen, this is a result of the delusion that costs are primarily related to transactions.

People who deliver services need no incentives or other external carrots and sticks. In an intelligent design they are intrinsically motivated, proud to do what they do. Whenever I take leaders to organisations where such a philosophy is embedded, they never fail to ask: "What did you do to the people?" The question reflects their command-and-control assumptions, because nothing was 'done' to the people. They work in a different system, and their leaders manage the system, not the people. In this environment staff 'light up'; their motivation is palpable.

As I have already mentioned, these systems have no 'back office'. They are services designed against demand. Where expertise is required that doesn't exist in the place of transaction, it is 'pulled' to the front line, not 'pushed' to a back office. Managers will say that this is unachievable, because they cannot conceive of front-line staff being capable of 'doing everything'. They are often surprised at how much people can do when they work in a system where they learn every day.

Together, these design principles provide a service system that is capable of responding to the variety of customer demand. More importantly, as demand changes so can the system, improving its sustainability. The designs look nothing like conventional command-and-control hierarchies.

Understanding the flaws in current assumptions and practices and how they lead us astray is the essential prerequisite of change for the better. For that, managers need to observe and study, the only way to help them unlearn what they currently believe. Change cannot be an article of faith; it has to be the result of gaining knowledge.

Chapter 8: Effective change starts with 'study'

Conventional management thinking says you can't start a change without a plan. But plans, cost-benefit analyses and the like are only guesses, frequently spurious, sometimes outright deceptions. You cannot know what will be achieved with a change before you make it because it is impossible to plot all interactions between the many variables involved; it is a folly to pretend that you can.

The changes to public services I shall describe here have resulted in levels of performance that managers would never have dared to countenance in any plan. For example, who would believe that you could improve stroke care and halve the costs? Who would believe you could deliver housing repairs to tenants on the day and at the time they want them and, similarly, dramatically reduce costs?

These results, and the others I shall describe, have been achieved by starting the change with 'study', understanding the 'what and why' of current performance.

The leaders of these services have followed the Vanguard Model for 'check', the first in an iterative three-stage improvement model (subsequent steps are 'plan' — where you design a better system and can predict improvement while not knowing by how much — and 'do' — where you implement the new design). The model was published in my 2008 book[1] and illustrations of its use in many public-sector services have been published on the internet, with tactics and guidance for users[2]. I reproduce an overview here:

The Vanguard Model for 'check'

The purpose of 'check' is to understand the 'what and why' of current performance as a system — how and why it gives the results it does.

The version of the model I shall present here is used in transactional services, which account for many public sector services.

The Vanguard Model for 'Check'

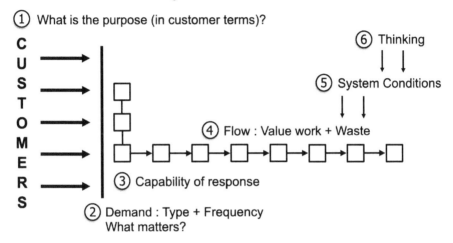

The Vanguard Model for 'check'

'Check' follows six steps:

1. What is the purpose?

The first question to address is: what is the purpose of this service, in the customer's terms? This is a vitally important step because in step 3 you will be measuring achievement of purpose *from the customer's point of view*, and these measures will be used in the redesigned service to control and improve performance. It is usually not difficult to articulate the purpose of a service from a customer's point of view, but if it is not immediately obvious, as is sometimes the case, park the question and return to it after step 2, which usually makes it much clearer.

2. What are the types and frequencies of demand (T+F)?

To understand demand, you have to study it, in customer terms, at every point of transaction: why do they call, what do they need, what would create value for them, what matters to them? It is impossible to move forward without having a thorough understanding of the major types of value and failure demands and their predictability. Value demands are the demands the service exists to meet; I defined failure demand earlier (Chapter 2). Distinguishing between predictable and unpredictable is also essential, a service designed to meet hard-to-predict demand would be impossibly complex. Similarly with things that go wrong, it is important to know what goes wrong predictably.

3. How well does the system respond to demand?

Having understood demand in customer terms, you now need to see how well the system responds in terms that matter to the customer (back to your statement of purpose). While the last step, studying demand, alerts managers to failure demand and is usually a surprise, this step, measuring achievement of purpose in customer terms, invariably administers a major shock. In flat contradiction to the message conveyed by management's existing measures-in-use, it reveals how poor their service really is for customers.

4. Studying flow

Only now, having understood demand and measured achievement of purpose from the customer's point of view, can you proceed to observe the flow of work.

When studying flow, it is important to observe certain rules. Do not ask people what they do; do not put people in a room and get them to write out the flow on 'Post-it' notes on the walls; do not read the procedures manuals; and certainly don't ask managers — they will be the least likely to know. The only way to build up an understanding of what is really going on is to follow a succession of individual pieces of work all the way through the system. As you do so, bear in mind that the work comprises just two elements: value work — work that contributes directly to meeting customer demand — and waste — everything else. That is the only definition of waste you will need[3].

5. Understanding system conditions

Waste (I prefer the term sub-optimisation) is man-made. It is a consequence of system conditions: measures, roles, process design, procedures, IT, structure, contracts and so on. The focus in this step is to understand the particular system conditions that are sub-optimising any particular service flow. This is important because the aim of the service redesign is to remove the causes of sub-optimisation.

6. Management thinking

Following the model for 'check' achieves two learning outcomes: you know the 'what and why' of performance as a system, and as your knowledge develops you realise that this means 'me too': the causes of sub-optimisation are all to do with the way we think. For example, we believe in targets, standards, procedures, controlling people and so on, but we discover that managing this way sub-optimises the flow of work which, in turn, reduces the capability of the system to do what customers need it to, and this, in turn again, generates quantities of failure demand and other costs. Conducting 'check' creates enormous energy for action — you can see what is wrong and you want to do something about it.

Seeing a service as a system

The outcome of studying the work in this way is a system picture that puts together everything that has been learned and which illustrates the dynamics of the particular service. Here I shall describe what has been learned in three public-sector examples, starting with housing repairs — some of whose features I described earlier.

Housing repairs

When managers investigate how often their service completes a repair to the tenant's satisfaction on the first visit (i.e. the achievement of purpose in customer terms), they discover that the success rate is generally less than 40%. Following up by asking how often the instructions to the tradesman (through the 'schedule of rates') match what is required, the answer is not very often. As well as sending the wrong diagnosis, it also often dispatches the tradesman with the wrong materials, so the job can't be done. Then managers discover that in these circumstances workers can only meet their activity targets (so many repair calls a day) by deploying their ingenuity to avoid being seen to fail: closing jobs that are not completed from the tenant's point of view or where they have been unable to gain access, prioritising jobs according to the need to meet targets and/or earn bonuses. Worse, many jobs require a number of activities (plumbing, carpentry, decorating), each subject to its own target. Hence the phenomenon of an organisation boasting that it has met all its individual targets while what the customer experiences is a routine repair that takes weeks or months to complete.

Studying the work reveals that there are a number of such constraining design problems (system conditions): work can't be reliably diagnosed over the phone by agents in a call centre; the Schedule of Rates, developed to control costs, does the reverse; buying materials on the basis of unit cost leads to materials being unavailable when needed; targets serve to distort the way work is done and bonuses or incentives for tradesmen motivate them to maximise their earnings, which is not the same as being productive. The aim of the redesign is to remove all these constraints.

Housing Benefits

The purpose of a benefits service is to pay the right money as quickly as possible to those who are eligible. Studying housing benefits usually reveals that it takes months and sometimes an extraordinary number of visits for claimants to get their benefits paid — which accounts for the frequency of signs warning people what will happen if they are abusive to staff. Managers discover that the measures in use — service standards and targets — give a completely misleading impression of the customer experience.

In housing benefits, failure demand typically accounts for up to 80% of all demand. As I noted earlier (Chapter 3), the design is a front-office, back-office model in which back-office staff take a different view of the claimant from those in the front. So they send out letters asking for things that were not required by front-office personnel. As with all back-office designs (see Chapter 3) one case can create a whole series of 'work tasks' because the flow of work is fragmented. Often electronic work objects get lost in the IT system; as few as 3% of claims go cleanly through the service.

By studying the flow of work, managers learn that their assumption that splitting work into functions to improve efficiency actually has the opposite effect; similarly the idea that service standards in the front office will improve service is shown to actually have the effect of driving incomplete work into the back office, only increasing rework and delays. Working to targets just exacerbates these problems.

IT help-desks

Many public services have IT help-desks. Most often they don't help! From the customer's point of view the purpose of a help-desk is to resolve a problem immediately (e.g. 'get me logged on') or, for some problems, resolve them as soon as possible (e.g. 'buy me a new computer'). Studying help-desks typically shows that little of the 'resolve-it-now' work is resolved at the first point of transaction and most of the 'as-soon-as-possible' demand takes an extraordinarily long time. Failure demand typically runs at well over 50%, the primary causes being the staffing of the first point of transaction by people with inadequate expertise and its corollary, keeping experts away from customers; work specialisation which, together with the inaccessibility of experts, creates a high number of handovers; a focus on activity — job tickets 'completed' (not the same as completing jobs from the customer's point of view) and the usual service-centre focus on service standards: picking up the phone, dealing with calls in limited times and working to service-level agreements.

Much as with the case of benefits processing, managers learn that their focus on activity and cost is actually driving up the volume of activity and, therefore, driving up costs. Managers now understand why their help-desk doesn't help.

It is important to note that in these examples, and indeed in all public services we have studied, the features found to be system conditions creating sub-optimisation were all treated by the regulators and trade associations as 'best practice'. I shall return to this subject in Chapter 22. But now we move on to what these services look like when they are redesigned.

Chapter 9: Better thinking, better design

To return to the fundamental principles I outlined in the introduction to Part 2, redesigning a transactional service consists, in short, of designing the service against customer demand. If we know what demands from customers are predictable, we can equip the front line with the wherewithal to serve them. Customers can easily 'pull value' from the system — i.e. get what they need — with the result that costs fall. The measures of achievement of purpose in customer terms are used by the front line, where the work is done, to control and improve performance, and by managers to improve the system, everything beyond the control of front-line workers.

When we think about designing services that work, we think about designing for perfection — what it would take to create a perfect service. Of course, perfection is hard if not impossible to achieve, but the aim is to get ever closer, and that requires the right roles and measures.

I shall give some examples of service redesigns using the same services described in the last chapter.

Housing repairs

Studying repairs shows that it is impossible make an accurate diagnosis of the requirement in a call centre. The only way to achieve an accurate diagnosis is to put a tradesman in front of the problem. Because the 'study' phase has identified what the predictable value demands are (i.e. what the properties predictably need), it is now possible do two important things: equip the tradesman with the expertise needed to diagnose and fix the problems, and ensure that he or she carries the requisite materials.

Since tradesmen are deciding what the job is, they are also best placed to determine how long it will take — a necessity in order know with confidence when they will be free to take another job. Any materials required that are not carried by the tradesmen are ferried to them, the principle being that tradesmen — the productive resource — should not be used for unproductive activity like fetching supplies from shops or stores.

Generally these designs begin with measures of end-to-end time, the measure first developed in the 'study' phase, but it soon becomes apparent that it is possible to deliver a repair on the day and at the precise time that suits the tenant, so *that* becomes the primary measure-in-use. Materials are measured on the basis of availability and time, not unit cost. By focusing on minimising the time that materials are in the system, material costs fall dramatically (I shall return to this in Chapter 22).

The consequences are a dramatic improvement in capacity — tradesmen are able to do more work — a dramatic improvement in first-time completions and a dramatic reduction in overall costs.

Housing benefits

If the purpose of the service is to inform people whether they are eligible and to pay those who are eligible quickly, that is what must be measured. Having knowledge of the predictable value demands ('I want to make a claim', 'I need to report a change in circumstances') front-line staff are equipped with the expertise to handle all predictable demands, enabling them to make rapid decisions about eligibility and pass eligible claims for immediate payment. In exceptional cases the employee 'pulls' help from someone who has the necessary expertise.

These simple principles always result in an astonishing reduction in end-to-end times and, as a consequence, happier claimants and much lower costs. Look at it this way: the value work required to establish eligibility and make a payment takes less than 30 minutes, which is what a perfect service would deliver. Of course, that's difficult in reality because many claimants will not know what is required of them, but the design described here is always moving the total in that direction. For comparison, the national target was set at 28 days, while the true end-to-end time for the Whitehall/DWP-promulgated 'best practice' design — complete with front office, back office, service standards and activity targets — was typically 52 days or more and took up to 10 claimant visits.

Most benefits offices that rethink the work on the new principles rapidly find themselves processing benefits in days rather than weeks — even while also experiencing increasing demand as a result of the recent recession[1].

IT help-desks

IT help-desks can significantly boost capacity, reduce operating costs and improve customer service (i.e. help!) by taking much the same route. Good knowledge of demand leads to better provisioning of expertise at the first point of transaction, typically leading to a rise in first-call resolution from as little as 10% to as much as 80%. Similarly, by designing the 'as-soon-as-possible' services to have minimal handovers, time-to-deliver resolution falls. In local authorities, both of these changes result in a massive drop in failure demand and an effective increase in capacity that, in turn, means fewer staff need to be employed (authorities typically drop contractor staff quickly). In one local authority demand on the IT help-desk increased by 52% after new systems were introduced, but an outstandingly improved service was delivered with 11% fewer personnel[2].

All of the above are transactional services (by which I mean they start with a customer demand). And that's the clue to success in the design of transactional services: understanding what customers need, in their terms, enables you to deliver a high-quality, low-cost service. Good service is, actually, much cheaper.

Implications for management roles

In all of these examples a key part of the change is a shift in the role of management. Conventionally managers see their job as managing people and budgets. In these radically better designs their job is to act on the system. For example, the key to all of these designs is the nature of demand. This decides what expertise is needed to solve customers' problems, so it becomes a major focus for managers. Rather than worry about demand in terms of volume, managers focus on demand in terms of type: what do we know about the predictability of demand, and is demand changing?

Given that good knowledge of demand is now the starting point for training front-line staff, another focus for managers is the quality of that training (how are we doing at equipping people with the expertise required, and can we improve this?). Some incoming demands are beyond the capacity of the front-line worker to handle, in which case he or she 'pulls help' rather than passing the work on. Management's focus becomes: when the front line 'pulls', how well does the help work from their point of view? If help has to be pulled regularly to meet certain types of demand, managers will see the need to move that expertise to the front line. It is the same philosophy that a repairs unit applies to materials: are they available as required?

Managers focus on measures that relate to the purpose of the services: the volume of work that can be completed at the first point of transaction and end-to-end times for work that requires more to be done than can be provided by a front-line service. As the primary controls are now employed in the work by those performing it, management's job is to focus on the system conditions beyond the control of the front line that need to be changed to effect improvement — effectively being enablers, breaking down organisational barriers. Working this way enables management to see the relationship between leading measures, the measures now in use, and lagging measures — the ones they no longer manage with (e.g. budget and productivity). They can see how costs fall by managing flow.

Profound results

These are just three examples of service redesign using the fundamental principles described earlier. We have published many others, all of which show similarly profound results. For example, in social care services we see dramatic reductions in administration and material provision (walk-in showers, grab rails, etc.), while fewer people are shunted into expensive care homes. In road repairs the number of potholes repaired in a working day has doubled or trebled. A stroke-care unit improved care and halved its costs while using fewer beds (leaders learned that managing beds, as is common practice in the NHS, actually drove bed utilisation up). Many other cases tell the same story[3].

Chapter 10: 'Locality' working

In the last chapter I described the redesign of housing benefits. What started to become apparent when we understood demand in customer terms was that people who were claiming benefits had other contextual needs — housing problems, family problems, alcohol or drug dependency problems, employment problems and the like. Although they attended the housing benefits office to claim benefits, their overarching need was for help to get their lives back in order.

   We found a similar situation in housing allocation services. When one local authority studied demand into its allocations and letting service, it quickly learned that 50% of those presenting would never be eligible and a further 35% had life problems which social housing would not solve, which left just 15% in genuine need of social housing[1].

   While this revealed the inanity of putting every applicant for social housing on a 'waiting list', even if they would 'wait' forever, it also brought to the surface human needs that were not being met. In response, the service changed the way it worked. Applicants who had no hope of being housed were helped to explore more suitable provision or relevant sources of help; those with life problems were helped to help themselves in resolving them. The genuinely needy group was appropriately housed, with support to deal with other contextual problems. The result was a dramatic reduction in the waiting list and a huge improvement in first-time resolution of presenting problems, to 80%, with no call on additional resource.

   The same approach was adopted by local authority benefits services (described in the last chapter), with similar results. People's contextual needs could be met with no extra resource, resulting in a reduction in demand into other public services.

This opened our eyes to an enormous opportunity. When we first started helping public-sector organisations to improve, our focus — taking what we had learned with private-sector clients — was on improving service delivery. While getting benefits or housing faster was beneficial, however, it was only a small step towards resolving the underlying life problems and issues of those receiving the individual service, whether care, housing or benefits. Helping people solve their contextual problems in benefits and housing allocations offices was a step forward — but even that was less than perfect, because for the problem to be solved it was necessary for those in need to present.

The next step in the progression was to understand demand in families and communities, and to go 'out' to understand it rather than waiting for it to appear in disparate services. We began, with all relevant local services participating (local authority, housing, police, fire and rescue, NHS, voluntary-sector services), to study what happens to all demand for what you might call 'my-life-has-fallen-off-the-rails' services.

People's lives fall off the rails in a variety of ways: infirmity, disability, family breakdown, drug or alcohol dependency, inability to manage finances and/or unemployment. What happens to people when their lives go wrong and they seek help from the state? You might think that in a civilised society someone would take time to understand the need and support them in getting back on track. But that's not what happens.

Instead, people are subjected to a series of assessments — a series because the majority of assessments lead to assessors referring people on to other assessors each of whom, in the recipients' eyes, asks much the same questions and looks at the person needing help through their own specialist lens. Many assessors tell people their needs are insufficient to warrant help from the service their function provides; budgets are protected using 'thresholds' to screen out people with what are seen to be insufficient needs (in adult social care this is called 'Fair Access to Care Services', FACS; 'fair' being a misnomer). Performance is managed by adherence to assessment and case-management targets.

Analysis reveals how the targets drive up referrals and the closing of cases, consuming valuable resources and doing nothing of value for people who need help. Also thrown into relief is the folly of the eligibility 'thresholds'. While managers think they will thereby husband scarce resources, in reality the effect is to delay the provision of help until people get worse, so that meeting their needs eventually costs much more. 'Study' reveals how many of the services provided are standardised and so fail to meet the variety of people's needs, consuming resources unnecessarily. If a service *is* delivered, it will probably have been commissioned. Commissioners purchase services by creating specifications against which providers bid on price, the objective being to obtain the lowest unit costs for the service specified. But the low unit costs are a delusion, because the standardised services fail to meet the variety of people's needs. If clients re-present with the same or, by now, exacerbated problems, they will often be offered exactly the same service again. If, as is sensible, they refuse it, since it was no help last time, they are likely to be labelled 'uncooperative'.

To return to the size of the opportunity: of the £695bn currently spent on public services, by far the largest chunk is spent on helping people whose lives have fallen off the rails. In local authorities — just one of the service-providers involved — care budgets are typically 20% of their expenditure[2]. Given the lessons of 'check', the best advice to give someone whose life has fallen off the rails is, 'sort yourself out', because the state may only make you worse. But there is a more positive way to look at this. The state currently consumes enormous resources to little useful end. So if we can design services that help people get their lives back on the rails, we not only increase human welfare — a good in itself — we will cut expenditure dramatically.

As ever, the key to achievement is a thorough knowledge of demand. In one geographic area comprising 2,589 households, it was found that 5% of the population were placing demands on multiple services. When participants from the agencies involved spent time with these families and individuals to understand their needs in context, it transpired that the majority of the problems were predictable. The highest-frequency issues were (percentages representing demand across all cases):

· Employment (67%)
· Managing finances (67%)
· Benefits and credits (42%)
· Suitability of housing (33%)

- Insecurity over housing status (29%)
- Distance from friends/relatives (25%)
- Drug/alcohol dependency (25%)
- Need for furniture (21%)
- Housing repairs (21%)

Working in multidisciplinary teams (in effect ignoring traditional functions), they visited every family making demands on public services, working to the following principles:

- To fully understand the person/family and the real problem that is to be solved
- To help the person/family identify solutions to their problems
- To help them to help themselves
- To 'pull' on (i.e. bring in) specialist expertise as and when required

The principles illustrate what was learned in the 'study' phase: the most important skills required are listening, understanding and helping people understand themselves. The provision of specialist expertise was then only applied where it was needed and where it was seen to be proportionate to actual needs, meeting the recipients' definition of a 'better' life.

Working this way, we could predict that demand would fall across other agencies. Tracking demand, the fall was quickly seen in children's services, anti-social behaviour units, police and debt services. More importantly, the families and individuals who were being helped gained in stability and ceased seeking help from public services. Estimates of the financial savings varied from 5% to 40% of operating budgets in the conventional services (we work to the principle that cost savings cannot be predicted and are emergent; conventional cost/benefit analyses are merely guesses and any guess could lead to sub-optimisation — e.g. meeting the plan by damaging the system). Having said that, one analyst has estimated that extrapolating the savings we have seen across the entire public sector could save in the order of £16bn[3].

The accuracy of the prediction is not the important thing. When the costs of individual cases traversing this new design are compared to previous expenditure patterns, large savings are a given. But much more importantly, as lives get back on track, overall demand falls. The result: happier individuals, better families, more functioning communities. Isn't that the purpose of public services?

This work has been labelled as 'locality' working. It was published in collaboration with Locality[4].

Coincidentally with publication of the Locality report, we learned of a similar approach taken by the state of Utah in the USA. How has Utah, a notoriously right-wing state, solved the problem of homelessness? It has decided that the financially responsible course is to give people homes. Those rehoused pay rent if they can and don't if they can't. But each one has the support of a caseworker to solve their other problems (i.e. the ones that caused them to be homeless in the first place), be they drug dependency, unemployment, family breakdown, mental illness and so on. The results bear out our own: much lower costs and less demand as fewer people experience problems, more people getting their lives back on the rails and, as they do, they begin to pay rent.

Many people will fear that this will simply encourage dependency. The opposite is the case. The Utah experience (the lessons of which are now being taken up by other states) corresponds to what we have learned in the UK: that the vast majority of people whose lives have fallen off the rails want to lead a normal (in their terms) life. Very few of them are, as politicians claim, 'scroungers'.[5]

Chapter 11: IT as pull, not push

We have seen how often IT systems fail when they are employed, as
is the norm, as the means for change, the thing you do first (build the
IT, train the people, implement the change). The perceived importance
of IT is reflected in the fact that major change budgets now sit in
IT departments in organisations. In both private- and public-sector
services these budgets have ballooned. Developing IT in a better
way shatters the need for large investments as well as dissolving the
problem of IT failure.

   We have to turn our thinking about IT development on its head.
Instead of IT being the driver of change, it is relegated to last in
the order of things. This approach has been developed with our
private-sector clients[1], and always following a change to their service
operations. Once new and better service operations are established,
leaders start to appreciate the fundamental errors in the way in which
IT has conventionally been employed. They know from experience that
the service improvements are independent of IT — indeed, to make
them some IT has had to be turned off and what has had to be retained
acts as a constraint rather than as an enabler.

'Study' — improve — pull IT

The first step is as I described in Chapter 8: 'study'. If IT is a major
component of a service operation, it is important to involve IT
development people in the 'study' phase, but with no brief to do
anything with the current IT. It is as far removed from conventional
business analysis as it is possible to be. Studying begins with no
articulation of the problem; in fact all current perceptions of problems

must be put to one side. No plan, no specification, no requirements other than the questions: 'What can we learn about the "what and why" of performance?' and, 'Can this be improved?' 'Study' reveals the causes of poor performance and the means for improvement.

The second step, improvement, also makes no demands on IT. The object is to take what is known from studying the service and improve the way it works (as described in Chapter 9). In the course of doing this any IT system in use may be either treated as something that has to be worked around or it may be put aside for the time being.

Only when the new service design is stable and demonstrably improved does attention turn to the IT developer's contribution; and the questions now are: 'What can IT do to help this new design work even better?', 'How can we hard-wire this better design?' and, of course, 'How do we turn off the current IT, if necessary?' The result is much less IT that is far more productive than previously.

Housing repairs

In conventional housing repairs designs, IT is used by call-centre agents to record tasks and their associated targets and schedule-of-rates decisions and to send tasks on to tradesmen. The IT is used by managers to monitor tradesmen's productivity, report on achievement of targets, control materials and so on. Such IT systems conventionally cost upwards of £250,000. In the 'study' step the folly of the service design becomes apparent — and is understood to be the major cause of poor performance (as illustrated in Chapter 8). The IT is the backbone of the service design, maintaining the system conditions, so when the service is redesigned it can be removed.

The 'improve' step creates a service design that puts the tradesmen in control and, when this new design is stable, the IT is used by tradesmen to control their availability (they tell the system how long jobs will take), by managers to purchase materials at the rate of consumption and to keep records of the work done once it is done (removing the need for re-work created by the previous design). These better IT systems cost far less — in the tens of thousands — and are central to achieving better performance[2].

The dynamics uncovered in housing repairs also apply to other asset-management systems including, for example, road repairs.

Development planning services

Studying local authority planning services reveals two major problems with IT. One is that the front end must be able to interface with the government portal allowing members of the public to submit, see and, potentially, comment on, planning applications. In practice whatever comes in through the portal has to be printed to enable planners to do their jobs, while everything that comes in by hand needs to be scanned in to the system.

The second problem is that 'IT solutions' for planning being sold by providers — often with deceptive names designed to convey the idea of efficiency — have the usual features that claim to 'control the flow' (they don't) which standardise procedures, require electronic work flow and drive handoffs (as well as the obligatory checking this causes), introducing delay and demoralising professionals. The IT system makes judgements on who should be consulted based on a set of rules, such as anyone who lives within a certain range. Since these mechanical rules take no account of the local reality, they invariably miss people who should be consulted and consult some who need not be (in one local authority consultation was found to be 90% wrong).

Since much of the initial work on the application is carried out by less experienced staff, driven by a flawed belief that this is more efficient and enabled/controlled by the IT, these omissions are only discovered and re-worked by qualified planners when the application finally lands on their desks. If the planners are working to targets, as many still do, a consequential problem is that this adding of consultees means they have to restart the consultation period (usually 14 days), even though for the overall target of 56 days the clock is still ticking. This added pressure to meet the arbitrary target conflicts with the true purpose of making a good decision. The primary management information provided by the IT is that needed for monitoring this target; extracting any other measures that will help to understand the performance in applicants' terms is incredibly difficult.

When planning is redesigned, the end-to-end times and individual planners' workloads (now the primary measures) fall, planner productivity increases, and applicants are delighted with what is now a helpful service[3]. Withdrawn applications drop (persuading applicants to withdraw applications and then resubmit them was one way targets were cheated), appeals drop and, as local agents start to see a change from the planners, the quality of applications improves.

Because the government portal is mandated it has to stay in place, but many features of the IT can be turned off or avoided, for example automated decisions about who needs to be consulted, letting the planners re-engage their brains and get on with the job of making a good decision.

Housing benefits

Many of the same features and problems are found in housing benefits administration. IT systems are conventionally used to pass electronic work from the front- to the back-office, to monitor service standards and the activity of the workers and to create reports on what is called 'work states' (usually, in truth, in a right old state), meaning how much work is where so that managers can move resources around to get work completed. Following a redesign, it becomes apparent that IT is only really useful for maintaining records of individuals' circumstances and payments, which can often be handled by inexpensive desk-top systems.

Care services

In care services, studying reveals how a national IT system — in this case the 'Integrated Care System' (ICS), another misnomer — has become the *de facto* purpose of the work: filling in forms and meeting deadlines for reports prompted by ICS, while the administrative reports generated then become a focus for regulators. On the other hand what matters to people receiving care is an understanding of what they themselves need and continuity of relationships, and ICS contributes absolutely nothing in that regard. On the contrary, 'study' reveals how ICS actually prevents carers seeing the whole person and understanding what is happening to people end-to-end, through the period of support. The IT forces care workers to complete records in a predetermined, standardised fashion, using questions whose nature and sequence are unconducive to the care relationship and ensure care services look at those who need help in a fragmented way. Because of this, important information is often missing, while irrelevant information is carefully captured with much duplication. All these things get in the way of understanding, and giving aid to, individuals. Instead, they increase the associated risks[4].

When social care is redesigned, the most important measure used in the work is a clear definition of what matters to the citizen, defined in conjunction with the individual, allowing achievement against purpose to be tracked during the period of support[5]. Systems which do that have been developed inexpensively by the staff providing the support, turning off the fields in ICS that are rendered redundant.

IT help-desks

In one local authority, IT managers decided to improve the incident management system used by the IT help-desk following ITIL guidelines on fault reporting[6]. In essence, this meant buying an incident-tracking system for logging incidents, keeping records of fault diagnosis and actions, automating the workflow and providing managers with status reports; an off-the-shelf software package of significant expense.

Following the 'study-improve-pull-IT' logic, they parked their plan and set about studying and improving the flow of work first, using their current job-logging system to record incidents and collect data to help them learn and improve: understanding the type and frequency of demand over time and measuring the capability of response by major types of demand, also noting and determining how best to employ the expertise required to solve predictable problems.

The improvements they quickly gained taught them they had no need for the software package which they could now see was primarily focused on problem-management; their new design focused on problem-solving rather than problem-management and had the right measures in place to ensure continuous learning and improvement.

Lower costs, higher value

The contrast between the IT resources needed in conventional IT-led change and the IT resources required to solve the real problem is nothing short of breath-taking. It is the route that IT development needs to go — but for obvious reasons it is unlikely to be the IT industry that takes the lead[7].

Part 3: Things that make your head hurt

Introduction

The management of service organisations is subject to a number of counterintuitive truths. In Part 2 I introduced one: that costs fall as service improves. This stands in direct contradiction to the conventional belief that the better the service or quality, the higher the cost.

This book features a number of other counterintuitive truths. Some appear simple, but are capable of being profoundly misunderstood, as happened when Whitehall developed an enthusiasm for the idea of managing demand (see Chapter 20).

In Part 3, I want to focus on a few counterintuitive truths that really make people's heads hurt, truths that are considered truly unconscionable.

Chapter 12: Targets and standards make performance worse

I have to begin with targets. In my 2008 book[1] I discussed all the arguments politicians bring forward in defence of targets: targets motivate people; targets make people accountable; the alternative is ambiguity and fudge; it is impossible to run services without them; all organisations have targets; targets enable comparison; 'unintended consequences' is the argument of those who seek to defend the status quo; if we don't have targets the wealthy will opt out of common provision and public services will become a shabby last resort for those who cannot afford anything better; and targets are fine if you do them right.

None of the arguments stands up. Some of the arguments show that people think 'no targets' means 'no measures', which is not the case. But it illustrates what's in their heads.

In that book I also discussed whether there is a reliable method for setting a target, the usual methods advocated being: base it on experience; set a 'stretch'; let the subordinate decide; and ask the customer. In short, there is no reliable method for setting a target.

Despite the coalition government's promise that targets will no longer be driven by Whitehall, they are alive and well in many public services. Targets are still thought of as a means to accountability, a favoured claim amongst politicians. But in truth they are a means to sub-optimisation. Ignorance is no defence, so if we must talk about accountability, shouldn't politicians be held accountable for causing people to act in ways that sub-optimise public services?

Targets and policing

In April 2014 the Metropolitan Police Federation reported on results of a survey of its members[2] that were described as 'devastating'. Police officers described a 'bullying' culture where they were targeted on the number of arrests they made and the number of stop-and-searches with a ratio of 'positive' outcomes. Failure to meet the target led to 'action-plans' for individuals with, in worst cases, the threat of misconduct procedures: "If you don't achieve your four arrests this month, then you're on a hit list and your managers will come and get you."

The reaction from a senior assistant commissioner was predictable. He described the report as "sensationalising", blaming the problem on a "small number of local managers" who held to the view that there was "small minority who don't like being held to account". He argued that accountability was the reason crime had fallen[3].

In a statement, the force said: "We are faced with many challenges, not least delivering improvements against the background of a reduced budget. However, despite this we do not recognise the claim that we have a bullying culture. We make no excuses for having a culture that values performance."[4]

But these are not 'performance measures' and this is not a culture that values performance — it is a culture that has internalised false ideas about measurement. (I'll come back to that.)

The Public Administration Select Committee added their voice to concerns about police data integrity, describing the under-reporting of crime driven by targets as reflecting the poor quality of police leadership[5]. Earlier Theresa May, the Home Secretary, had scrapped centrally-imposed police targets but acknowledged that performance measures were being reintroduced by some forces as a "security blanket". The report shows how they are an 'insecurity blanket', driving fear not confidence[6].

At about the same time that this story hit the news, the UK Statistics Authority withdrew the 'gold standard' status from police figures for reasons of "accumulating evidence of unreliability", a euphemism for cheating[7]. It is also no surprise that the regulator, the Chief Inspector of Constabulary, has described the cheating as only a "degree of fiddling" and has ruled out "institutional corruption"[8].

This is how the conventional mind deals with the dissonance created by people speaking the unspeakable. We have heard the same thing for years: misbehaviour around targets is limited to the few bad apples; targets are important for driving improvement and accountability. But stories of cheating the numbers are ubiquitous; targets drive people's ingenuity in other directions than improvement; 'accountability' strips people of discretion, judgement and responsibility.

Targets in health

In the latter days of the last Labour government I met Duncan Selbie when he was the Director General of Programmes and Performance for the NHS and the man responsible for 'Selbie's six' — the priority targets for health service managers which, if failed, were seen to be a "P45 offence"[9]. He had read my 2008 book and said he thought that when compared to what I had described in local authorities, the health service was far less target-driven. As we began to study health systems, we learned that in fact the NHS has far greater dysfunction created by central controls, and targets in particular.

Hospitals fiddle their figures for death rates. If deaths are coded as 'palliative' cases, they don't count towards hospital mortality statistics because they are classed as expected deaths[10].

Accident & Emergency (A&E) departments hold patients in ambulances, put patients in 'medical assessment units' and create space in the hospital by kicking out patients not ready to leave or cancelling planned admissions, all to avoid breaching the four-hour wait-time target.

Compounding the error, the Department of Health (DoH) fines hospitals for readmissions. To do so requires the setting of a time boundary (fixed at 30 days from previous discharge, an arbitrary number). In 2014 it was reported that readmission penalties totalled £390m[11]. Hospitals find ways to cheat, for example giving 'new' reasons for admission or simply not recording patients as readmitted.

Hospital managers complain that often the reasons for readmission are beyond their control, for example dehydration in care homes: the DoH reacts with new rules requiring commissioners to conduct clinical reviews with providers to determine the incidence of avoidable readmissions and to fine hospitals when the cause is a failure in community or social services[12].

It has become a veritable industry, consuming enormous resources to no positive effect (how can fining trusts help?) — to this we can add the harmful effects on patients and costs alike of working to targets and arbitrary measures.

The volume of attendances in A&E departments has been rising. As a consequence many hospitals are failing to meet the four-hour wait-time target. You may, as I do, wonder why four hours, why 95%? Leaving NHS Direct aside (as it won't provide direct access to an expert), A&E represents the last remaining point of access to the health service that is unconstrained: you can simply turn up. GP surgeries now constrain access through appointment systems. Rather than understanding what is driving attendances in A&E up and to try to solve the waiting-time target 'problem', politicians think we should provide alternative access to health services; hence NHS Direct, walk-in centres, more resources in GP surgeries. Politicians also think we should focus on the 'exit block' problem — the things that keep people in hospital and stop them vacating their beds. Some argue that the problem has been caused by ministers removing social-care support from the elderly and making it harder to make GP appointments. To tackle the problem DoH introduced the 'emergency rate tariff', under which hospitals receive reduced payments when emergency admissions are higher than expected. The scheme has cost trusts more than £700m since 2010, but emergency admissions have continued to climb[13].

Apparently wanting it both ways, DoH crows about the volumes of patients seen in A&E, describing it as a "testament to the hard work of staff"; and government acts to "strengthen the links between GPs and elderly patients, investing £3.8bn to join up health and social care"[14].

But we don't need any investment, as I demonstrate in this book. We don't have a resource problem; we have a design problem. What does anyone know about NHS demand? How much of the demand on A&E is failure demand? How much of this is created by the way health and care services are currently managed?

The failure to understand demand is exemplified by the 'Darzi walk-in centres' debacle. Because centres were opened with no knowledge of predictable volumes, many contracts were later terminated, at vast cost to the public purse, because of insufficient demand[15].

To have any chance of improving the system, we would need to know about the type and frequency of demand as well as volumes. Lacking any such elementary information, the NHS is being driven out of control by targets and investments in plausible remedies for the problems being created.

Everyone — ministers, think tanks, NHS managers, local authority care-service managers — parrots the assertion that demand is rising. It isn't. In every case we have studied so far, we have learned that demand is stable; demand for adult care support is stable, acute demand into hospitals is stable. When you tell that to civil servants and politicians, they think you are mad. I always ask them to produce the data. The data they always refer to is epidemiological, from which projections have been made. That won't help anyone improve the system. Only knowledge of actual demand will do that. What is rising, inexorably, is failure demand.

The way the health service thinks about demand illustrates the same problems as I described in Part 1. All demand is treated as 'work to be done', ignoring the important phenomenon of failure demand; treating demand as work to be done creates a focus on provision; the 'supply' side of the equation. Thus attendances at A&E and volumes of work going through specific treatment centres are used as the basis for determining what to 'supply'. However, as with care services and acute conditions (above), when we study new outpatient and primary-care demand we learn that it is stable. The system amplifies demand by the way it works: pathways, thresholds, quality outcomes frameworks (QUOFS), technology and the pervasive standardisation and fragmentation of service create more (failure) demand. So when we hear the argument that demand is rising, what it means is supply is rising. It is an elegant horror: the tactics employed to make supply more 'efficient' (e.g. standardisation and specialisation) are the causes of increasing failure demand. The health service is caught in the monstrous perpetual motion machine I described earlier (Chapter 4), needing to run faster and faster to keep up with the demand caused by trying to run faster.

As with industrialised services described in Part 1, the better alternative is to manage value not cost. To take a discrete example: on analysis, stroke incidence in one hospital proved to be as regular as clockwork. Knowledge of the predictability of demand by type enabled the service to be redesigned, providing a much improved service to stroke patients (and their relatives) at half the cost. As a consequence of the redesign, bed utilisation fell and fewer beds were required[16]. It is a further illustration of the counterintuitive mantra: managing costs (in this case of the NHS 'bed management') increases costs (more beds used); managing value drives down costs (fewer beds required).

In this and other cases, it becomes obvious when studying the system, that 'managing beds' (they have bed managers in hospitals and targets for 'length of stay') actually drives bed utilisation up. Why do we make hospital beds a constraint in a health system? Isn't that the last thing you would want to do?

The report by Robert Francis on the unnecessary deaths at Mid Staffordshire NHS Foundation Trust[17] acknowledged the adverse influence of targets, but accepted them as a normal and necessary means of control, rather than seeing the consequences as a reason to re-think the theories of control in use. In his recommendations, he argued that inspection for compliance will drive sufficient fear amongst healthcare professionals to improve — yet in his analysis he pointed to a fear culture that is already pervasive and dysfunctional. It is as though we can drive out fear by putting up posters: 'No fear here'. Francis didn't understand why there is a culture of fear.

A systemic relationship

There is a systemic relationship between purpose (what a service exists to do), measures (how performance is managed), and method (how people work in the system). Describing the relationship as systemic is to say that it is at work in every organisation, whether for good or bad, whether it knows it or not. The imposition of any arbitrary measures, such as targets, standards, service-level agreements, budget management, etc., replaces the real purpose of the system with a new *de facto* one, which is to meet the targets. As a result, method is constrained as the work is designed around reporting requirements. And this is the point: if you drive any arbitrary target number down a hierarchy you will engage people's ingenuity in finding ways to meet the target and make the numbers, which is not the same as improving performance. The problem is not only ubiquitous, it is systemic.

On the other hand, when measures are derived from purpose (from the customer's point of view) and are used where the work is done, method is liberated.

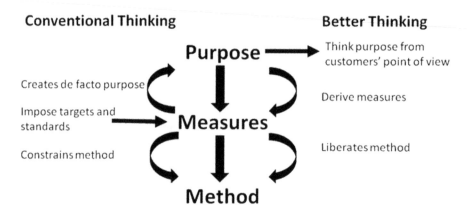

Conventional Thinking **Better Thinking**

Think purpose from customers' point of view

Creates de facto purpose

Derive measures

Impose targets and standards

Constrains method

Liberates method

Purpose → Measures → Method

Purpose, measures, method: a systemic relationship

Looking at the figure above, Chapter 8 described the first, dysfunctional relationship with three examples. Chapter 9 used the same examples to show how actual, rather than arbitrary measures, related to purpose and put into effect where the work is done, enabled those doing the work to understand and improve the services they were delivering. The test of a good measure is: does it help to understand and improve the work? All arbitrary measures fail that test. Measures that relate to purpose, used where the work is done, pass the test. To determine what better measures will help in understanding and improving performance, it is essential to study the system, in particular its purpose. I shall return to policing to illustrate this:

Choosing measures to improve the system

Recall my description of a conventional police control centre (Chapter 2), where a 'take-one — label it — ship it' design, passing activity around the innumerable functions lying behind it, stuffs the system with wasteful activity. To replace it with a system that is focused on achievement of purpose rather than meeting service levels, we need to start from a different point of view.

The purpose of policing is to prevent and detect crime and disorder, and provide reassurance to the community. We should think of the first point of transaction (the control centre) as a place that is highly sensitive to important calls related to crime and intelligence, but also service-orientated in respect of other more routine calls. For the latter, the ideal is to have as many calls as possible handled at that first point of transaction, providing exemplary service to the caller and, importantly, not filling other functions with activity. In this way, resources can be freed up to do the important work of detection and prevention.

This can only be achieved with thorough knowledge of demand — which thus becomes a key measure. It is essential for determining the expertise needed in the control room to solve problems at first pass, and for understanding the type and frequency of problems in communities. With accurate knowledge of hotspot locations, offenders and victims, the frequency of repeat problems becomes clear, which in turn makes it possible to focus resources effectively.

Solving more problems on the spot in the control room liberates other resources from procedural bureaucracy, increasing capacity for attending and investigating incidents. It also prevents important demand from being swamped by the less important in 'work queues', as was previously the case. The immediate consequences can be seen clearly; the volume of 'tasks' sent to local police stations and centralised functions drops dramatically.

Attending and investigating crime and disorder are core work flows. To improve the flow of work we need to know the end-to-end time from incident reports to officer attending, the end-to-end time from incident reported to investigation concluded, and the frequency of one-stop resolution by officers attending incidents. These are measures that relate to purpose; other things being equal, the better (shorter) the measures, the better the service.

Many investigations require forensic work. During the 'study' phase, police officers are often shocked to learn that forensic scientists are routinely deployed to some scenes of crime where they can add no value to the investigation, often deployed in order that the police can be seen to be doing everything to investigate, particularly when the crime is one that is monitored for 'victim satisfaction'. As a consequence, forensics resources become stretched so that in other cases investigation is limited or delayed. Also they learn that because the current emphasis in the prosecution service is all about ensuring that cases brought to court do not fail, again many forensic investigations are undertaken that add no value to the decisions and only serve to clog up forensic services. It is worth noting that the current drive to outsource forensics will keep the expertise away from where it is needed and will predictably diminish its value while driving up its costs.

To improve, we need to know the value of forensic activity to the investigation and the time it takes from receiving a request for forensics to the results being available. When forensics experts work alongside police officers, more informed decisions can be taken regarding forensic involvement, improving the quality of its contribution to investigations and thus convictions.

The same is true for intelligence, which should be an essential support for effective policing. 'Study' generally reveals how intelligence is analysed away from the core work — resulting, for example, in officers being sent out to do tasks knowing what to do but not why, patterns being missed and responses delayed — rather than where it can be used most effectively. For policing that better meets its purpose, we need to focus on the quality and utility of intelligence in detecting and preventing crime.

These better measures focus everybody on how well the policing system works; they can be used to understand and improve. The ultimate measure of improvement is the frequency with which problems in the locality are solved, resulting in a reduction in demand from communities. Isn't reducing demand — reducing criminal activity and disorder — the purpose?

Measuring and managing flow

It may help to think about the problem this way. What I have been illustrating in this book is that good service and lower costs are consequences of better, smoother management of the flow of work from and back to the customer. It is to manage outside-in. If anything occurs that causes workers in that flow to focus their attention upwards, to meet the demands of the boss, rather than horizontally, to meet the demands of the customer, the flow will be distorted and the system destabilised.

Managing with arbitrary measures — targets, standards, service-level agreements and the like — can only distort the system — impede the flow of work — and thus will only ever increase costs. Meeting the measures is quite different from improving performance; it means looking good, not being good. Picking up the phone in three rings is not as important as what happens when contact is made; meeting targets — or any arbitrary measure — can only lead to sub-optimisation of performance. Managing with measures that help you understand and improve the flow of work will lead to improvement.

Chapter 13:
Inspection can't improve performance

Many years ago, I worked with Pat Rattray, a leader in an insurance company's service centre in Edinburgh. When the study phase of the work was completed, this is how Rattray addressed her staff: "We used to take people off the street, train them in the things we thought they ought to know, not what the customers want them to know, then we told them to comply with procedures, adhere to scripts and keep within standard times. Then we had the audacity to inspect them to tell them where they went wrong. It is us who went wrong."

A powerful lesson for politicians and, for that matter, all leaders: when you learn you are wrong, say so, unequivocally. It generates enormous respect. Rattray had learned the folly of inspection, as well as understanding how the system governed her people's behaviour (more on this in Chapter 15). At the beginning of the assignment, she had asked me to take a view on her planned new inspection regime. She was proud that under the new arrangements the number of elements inspected was substantially reduced. When the study phase was completed, on the other hand, she could see that doing less of the wrong thing was still doing the wrong thing.

When you call a call centre you will often hear a recorded message: 'These calls are being recorded for training and quality purposes'. Service organisations have spent vast fortunes on call-recording equipment and deploy much of first-level management's time on 'one-to-ones' where the hapless worker gets feedback from his or her manager. First-level managers think this is an essential task; often they pride themselves at being good at this process. To help them unlearn — to see the folly of their ways — we sometimes ask them to take the 'error' data and plot it in a capability chart (in other words, to study measures over time[1]). What they always learn is that errors are low-level and stable; an entirely predictable part of the system. In short, all that time and money spent on inspection and feedback in the name of improving quality actually achieves nothing.

Engendering fear

Specifying the detailed content and order of a telephone call produces fear in service agents because if they get it wrong and the call is inspected, they are for the high jump. That is why call-centre agents often ask, 'Is there anything else I can do to help you today?' when you have just vented your spleen about something. In one big supermarket chain check-out staff are obliged to ask whether a customer needs help, as though he or she were incapable of making the judgement. (I always say, 'Do I look as though I need it?')

The philosophy of specifications and inspection is a disease. It gave rise to the popular (among managers) notion of 'mystery shopping', having people pretend to be customers, armed with checklists of what managers want to see in the transaction. But this is the mistake of focusing upwards rather than horizontally: is what managers want to see the same as what customers want to experience?[2]

In call centres, making agents work to specifications merely makes the experience customer-insensitive and drives up failure demand. In public-sector services, the philosophy of specification and inspection goes far beyond appraising (blaming) front-line workers. Every public service we have studied is obliged to work to specifications, whether targets or methods, dreamed up by Whitehall and regulators. For example, during the last Labour government the Audit Commission bullied councils to draw up plans for sharing back offices in benefits processing; the Commission for Social Care Inspection obliged care services to report on a whole series of measures that did nothing for achievement of purpose[3] (in fact they worked against it); planning departments were mandated to report on adherence to their 56-day target for deciding applications, effectively driving up refusals and approvals with conditions, making the process longer and more unwieldy for applicants[4]; today public services are ordered to share 'back-office' functions, and so on.

In these specification/inspection regimes, the inspector's role is to inspect for compliance. Failure to comply is a career-limiting move, resulting in a culture of fear.

The problem of validity

In our work with public services, a startling and consistent finding is that there is no material difference in terms of performance between a 'four-star' and a 'one-star' service. Whatever the ranking, levels of failure demand, ability to achieve purpose and system conditions governing performance are all pretty much the same. So what determines the official ratings? The answer is management's ability to present a good story about compliance, backed up with copious documentation for all of the things the inspector wishes to see.

When the problem of validity is too difficult to ignore, as with Haringey children's services, where a highly-rated department was manifestly unable to protect a vulnerable child in its care[5], and Mid Staffordshire NHS Foundation Trust, where a hospital approved by the inspectors as a highly-rated service was found to have an unacceptably high mortality rate[6], politicians assume that the problem is the quality of inspection rather than the inspection regime itself. When such shocking events occur, ministers commonly order a further inspection which duly downgrades the performance rating, unwittingly underlining the scope for inspection to be used as a political instrument.

We regularly hear pronouncements by ministers, regulators and other commentators that there are poor teachers/nurses/doctors/local authorities out there; it can only inculcate a culture of fear. This is what we do to public-sector professionals: vast resources are spent on their training and recruitment, and once they are in the job they find that someone else has been appointed to instruct them what 'good' looks like. Worse, because control is exercised by inspectors and regulators, all exercise of initiative is ruled out; anyone daring to act outside requirements is more likely to attract retribution than reward.

Consider the resources consumed by inspection activities: the costs of creating specifications, training inspectors to inspect for compliance, inspection itself, being inspected (including voluminous paperwork that inspectors expect to see, regardless of its value to the enterprise), and mock inspections to prepare for the dreaded visit —

all to no purpose other than to provide the regime with its arbitrary requirements. The largest costs associated with inspection are those caused by the imposition of specifications that themselves guarantee sub-optimisation, and, the poisonous icing on this dysfunctional cake: compliance that prohibits innovation.

Investing in preparatory inspection to stave off failure is apparently not limited to public-sector managers. When Michael Gove was Education Secretary, private education advisers were allegedly hired to monitor free schools at risk of failing and to do what was required to prevent a negative report from Ofsted, the schools inspectorate. It is to add another layer of inspection and control, using ingenuity to prevent political embarrassment to the minister at the expense of education as a whole[7].

Prevention beats inspection

Manufacturers learned back in the 1950s that inspection is too late; it comes after the errors have been made. To this day, it is not uncommon in manufacturing to find that more effort is spent at the end of the production line fixing mistakes than in getting things right the first time. It is prevention, not inspection, that improves performance — increasing the capability to make things right the first time.

What does this mean in something as simple as a call centre? The approach I outlined in Chapter 9 serves as an illustration. Front-line workers are trained against demand; in Rattray's example, they are equipped to deal with the demands that customers will predictably make on the organisation. They take responsibility, 'pulling' help when they need it. In case of service failure, managers firstly assume there is a fault in the system, in the ways in which workers are trained and supported, rather than blaming the worker. Failures in service are easily visible because front-line supervision is close to the work, rather than in a remote office conducting useless one-to-ones.

I devoted much of my 2008 book[8] to examples of how specifications cause sub-optimisation. Here is another that illustrates the differences between inspection and prevention.

Food safety

The first time Vanguard helped a council to investigate food safety, we learned it was regulated in the following way. Food-handling premises (restaurants, manufacturers, etc.) are visited according to a schedule and code of practice specifying the procedures council-employed inspectors must follow in each visit. Businesses are visited without prior warning. Much of the inspectors' time is spent preparing for visits, ensuring they have the right paperwork and checklists, with as little as possible communication with on-site workers during the visit. Following the visit, the inspector writes a report, listing any breaches of legislation, which is sent to the owner of the business. All inspection activity is reported to the regulator (the Food Standards Agency), and managers' focus is on adhering to the schedule. Falling behind will be reflected in the council league table and attract the attention of the regulator.

Studying revealed that inspectors had no knowledge of how working to this specification achieved the real purpose (keeping food safe) and showed that more than half their time was spent on administration (form-filling, report writing and so on). The relationship with food-business managers was adversarial. Many 'breaches', while real according to the letter of the law, were trivial and seen as nit-picking (e.g. training records not being up to date). Focused only on avoiding being singled out for falling behind schedule, food-safety managers would deliberately not add new businesses to the schedule if they were in danger of getting behind.

Redesign of the service focused on purpose: what does it take to make sure that food is safe? Businesses were visited without preparation and checklists, the inspectors talked to everyone and took action on the spot to explain and, if necessary, demonstrate safe practice. Food safety inspectors are highly trained; in this design they were able to bring their knowledge to bear directly where the work was done. Their approach was to help businesses keep food safe, not catch them out. Theirs is now a vocational role, the very thing they trained for.

The consequence is a far better relationship between inspectors and business owners, who now call for advice and help. Inspectors assess risk on a case-by-case basis and agree with the owners when to visit again[9].

Better food safety is just one tangible example of the benefits of shifting from a specifications/inspection regime to a prevention regime. Instead of being driven by fear, food-safety officers are driven by vocation, motivated to prevent risk, not motivated to avoid retribution by doling it out to others. I shall return to replacing inspection with prevention in Chapter 28.

Chapter 14: Regulation is a disease

Inspection, examination for conformance, is one element in the way public services are regulated. The other side of the coin is how the rules that people are expected to conform to are determined. This was something that became part of the Audit Commission's brief, making the inspector the arbiter. Regulation is thus a means for control. We have to question whether and how well it does that.

Every state in the European Union has a 'better regulation' task force, testimony to politicians' discontent with the cost and value of regulation. The task forces have been active over the last few years; in essence the quest of such task forces for 'better' has been to canvass regulators on what better regulation might look like using a process that was, by all accounts, time-consuming and bureaucratic. Because of the cost and the fact that it got nowhere, EU politicians are not extending the funding. But the problem hasn't gone away, and we should assume that the last people to come up with the right answer will be the regulators themselves. Regulators now talk of 'robust' regulation and 'intelligent' regulation, but show no understanding of why regulation is problematic in the first place.

When things go badly wrong in the public sector, as they do with all too alarming frequency, politicians often put the blame on regulatory failure. This is not entirely accurate. A better diagnosis is that it is a failure of the system, of which regulation is a central part. All of the features of poor service design I have described are due at least in part to regulation. The failures can be simply irritating, like dealing with call centres that are not citizen-friendly, experiencing a poor repairs process or having to go through the mill to get a planning permission; they can be exasperating when we learn, for example, that our local council has thrown money away on false economies such as outsourcing; they can be truly shocking when people suffer or die as a result of lack of care. Despite the widespread evidence of such failures, politicians persist in their conviction that regulation is beneficial and justifiable.

Regulators bring theory

The heart of the problem is that regulators bring with them their own theories of management and control. To take an example from the private sector: I know, because we have studied it, that the extensive mis-selling of financial services is driven by incentives, and when those incentives are removed, sales (genuine sales of honest products) go up — and the same is true for any other sector. Sales incentives act like any other target, distorting behaviour by creating a new, *de facto* purpose. In fact, the adverse consequences of incentives go beyond fewer sales: cooperation between salespeople withers, turnover of sales staff rises (often customers leave with them), and customer satisfaction falls.

Like conventional leaders in financial services organisations, regulators start from the assumption that without incentives salespeople won't sell. So the default regulatory position is that incentive schemes are fine provided that they are "well managed and can benefit [the firm's] customers"[1].

I have already described how, principally but not exclusively through the Audit Commission, regulation of local authority services is at the heart of their sub-optimisation. Regulators believe in targets, back offices and activity reporting and oblige the regulated to conform to their ideas about methods to be employed and measures to be used. Regulators are part of the problem, even at the heart of the problem, but they are not *the only* problem. They serve to propagate and sustain a disease. Here are three examples:

1) To return to housing benefits services, the Audit Commission promulgated service standards, front and back offices, activity management and targets as 'best practice'. Unfortunately they are not at all best, in fact all of these features are repeatedly revealed to be causes of sub-optimisation. Hence the widespread experience, endlessly puzzling to politicians, of services that tick all the regulator's boxes, yet offer poor quality at sky-high cost.

A local authority in the North West was awarded 'beacon status' — a status conferred by the regime to encourage others to visit for the purpose of industrial tourism. According to reports on the chief executive's desk, 80% of citizens' calls were handled 'one-stop'. Studying revealed that the definition of 'one-stop' in use was, 'We can't do any more with it'. Taking the citizens' view of one-stop revealed the real figure to be less than 15%.

Local councillors have been persuaded or bullied by Whitehall to outsource services. Trusting the plausible arguments and having no experience in the matter, they turn to outsourcing companies for guidance. As we have seen, many of these ventures are subsequently unpicked at significant cost; yet the ventures gained a tick from regulators, and the unchallenged consensus is that the failings are not with the idea but its implementation.

This problem is everywhere, and its cause is the regulator importing unfounded theory (or rather prejudice) about what good should look like.

2) What follows is the most shocking example of regulation sub-optimising public services we have found.

Many years ago Camphill Village Trust (CVT) established a number of communities to serve the needs of people with mental health disabilities. 'Residents' lived in communities with 'co-workers', volunteers who worked in exchange for board and lodging; they were what you might call therapeutic communities, for example running farms where everybody worked, contributing according to their abilities.

Since the last Labour government, the political narrative in social care heavily emphasises personalisation, choice and 'independent living' over separate communities, which are now looked on with suspicion. The Camphill establishments became a regulatory responsibility of the Care Quality Commission, and when the regulators arrived they didn't like what they saw. They didn't see that these were prospering communities giving residents and co-workers a constructive purpose and a happy life; instead they saw a lack of what they considered to be 'best practice', such as record-keeping and demonstrable knowledge of safeguarding regulations. The consequence was a series of damning reports on the CVT communities.

Acting through fear, the board of trustees brought in professional managers, largely from the NHS, whose task it was to 'up the game' to satisfy regulators. Volunteers felt crushed by the management factory that landed above them, issuing edicts which to the volunteers' minds made no sense. Many left, many were squeezed out. Managers brought in paid professional care workers (increasing costs) who knew how to write treatment plans, never considered necessary in the community and understandably viewed as a bureaucratic exercise by those who spent every day doing what seemed best for the people they helped.

The professionals introduced 'choice'. Residents, they noticed, didn't watch TV; instead evenings were spent engaging everyone in activities. Offered the choice, residents chose to watch TV in their own rooms. Some of the community got up early to milk the cows. Offered the choice, residents chose to have a lie-in. The milking herd had to go. When offered the choice of what to eat, residents chose sweets over healthy food, and obesity became a problem.

A vibrant and worthwhile community, a vehicle of vocation for idealistic co-workers and passionately supported by relatives and residents, was transformed into a 'shuffling' community that has increased its use of psychotropic drugs; residents in a position to leave started drifting away[2].

But at least CVT can now get a tick from the regulator.

3) The tragic events in Mid Staffordshire NHS Foundation Trust and in children's services in many local authorities represent the tip of the iceberg of healthcare systems failure. Recommendations from the many inquiries all amount to doing the wrong thing righter, strengthening regulation rather than re-thinking it.

The Francis report into the Mid Staffs tragedy[3] is a mass of detail: hugely disturbing detail — you can't fail to be moved by the evidence. But perhaps because he has a legal mind, Francis consistently fails to get behind the facts, leaving underlying assumptions unchallenged and never even opening the door to matters of theory. As a consequence his recommendations represent single-loop thinking[4]. The NHS is already subject to a massive burden of regulation, but Francis recommends more. He wants a 'zero tolerance' approach to breaches of fundamental standards, but never questions why the system as currently managed might produce such neglect. He calls for a culture that puts patients first, without stopping to consider why the current system does not.

If it is true that we have reached a level of dystopia that requires us to articulate a 'structure of clearly understood fundamental standards' — Francis's top recommendation — despair really is in order.

Coalition health secretary Jeremy Hunt took up Francis's theme of excessive box-ticking, bureaucracy and burdensome regulation to announce the setting up of a talking-shop for regulators and the regulated whose purpose was to reduce the regulatory burden by one third[5]. Why one third? Is it the right third? Why is it not two thirds? What value does box-ticking achieve? Hunt said, echoing Francis, that we need a culture that puts the patient first, not knowing how the current system obstructs any attempt to do that.

David Cameron waded into the fray, promising that the Francis report would be handed over to the police to find those to blame and also promising performance-related pay for nurses, the sack for the 'bad ones' and the obligation for all of them to fill in forms to prove they have spoken to every patient every hour[6].

Closing one of his presentations with a literary flourish, Hunt declared: "Let me finish with words from T.S. Eliot we should not forget, when he said, 'It is impossible to design a system so perfect that no one needs to be good'"[7]. I am no literary expert, but when I read Eliot's 'Choruses from the Rock', I experience a man regretting society's alienation from God; in the NHS, alienation from a worthy purpose: "What have we to do but stand with empty hands and palms turned upwards in an age which advances progressively backwards?"

Eliot (writing in 1934) describes how man faces a tremendous flood of meaninglessness because context has been removed. Man has created an artificial world based on the new gods of reason, money and power. This is exactly what has happened in health, the minister and his predecessors being responsible for a system that worships false gods, a system that is being regulated to death.

Politicians find it very difficult to renounce regulation. They frequently declare their desire to reduce red tape, but nothing much happens, at least in the public sector. It is the same at the level of the EU, where politicians insist that only regulations that have been specifically identified can be removed (for my part top of the list would be public-sector procurement — see Chapter 22). The difficulty is that politicians believe they must be seen to care. If they abolish a regulation it might look as if they don't care about whatever it is the regulation is supposed to stop: hence the persistence of regulatory creep.

But it is not a question of changing or improving regulation, as many people think. What is needed is a re-think of the entire philosophy. Regulations can only be justified if the rules have economic and social value, and further, that the economic cost of regulating doesn't exceed the economic cost of being regulated. This is what the 'better regulation' task forces should have had as their primary concern, the relationship between the value of regulation and its cost. They would have had to face the fact that currently the costs — knowable and unknowable — far exceed the value and in many cases detract from and/or provide no value whatsoever.

By imposing bad theories of management, regulators make services worse. Regulators developing better theories of management is not the answer, since regulation through adherence to specifications will still have the adverse effect of creating a culture of compliance.

I shall return to regulation to describe the principles that would considerably reduce the economic costs and, more importantly, foster innovation rather than compliance — that is, create value — in Chapter 28.

Chapter 15: It's the system, not the people

The quality theorists teach that more than 95% of the causes of performance are attributable to the system, the remaining 5% to the people who work in it[1]. If that is true (and it is), imagine the implications for all the 'people management' activities carried out in organisations: performance appraisal, motivational programmes, staff surveys, culture audits, managing the poor performer, and the like. Imagine the futility of phrases like 'our people are our most important asset', 'putting people first' and 'quality means you!' But that's how it is. So much of management's attention is directed to the 5%, not the 95%. It is the reverse of what is required: an almost entire waste of time, energy and talent.

In Chapter 3 I introduced what I call the 'core paradigm' in service management. Managers of service organisations are trained to concern themselves with the volume of work, the number of staff, and the time it takes to do things. From this it seems logical for managers to monitor employees' activity, reduce the time tasks take by setting standard times or moving work to computers, or installing interactive voice machines (press 1 for this, 2 for that). But all these steps are to do with optimising the use of people, sweating resources, in other words acting on the 5%. When managers treat all demand as work to be done, they miss the most important lever, understanding demand and discovering how much of it is failure demand. To standardise the work is to prevent the system from absorbing variety, so that costs can only rise.

Think back to the example of housing repairs (Chapters 8 and 9). The tradesman's ability to complete a repair on the first visit depends on having the right information, the right materials and the right skills. How much of that is to do with the tradesman? Yet what is managed is the tradesman's activity (jobs per man per day). I'm sure some readers will be thinking that the tradesman's skills are down to the tradesman — but isn't ensuring that he has the *right set* of skills a responsibility of management?

Recall also the case of housing benefits processing (Chapters 8 and 9). The causes of poor performance are service standards, activity management and the division of work between the front and back office. How much of that is in the control of the worker? Think back to Pat Rattray in her service centre (Chapter 13), imposing time constraints for calls, working to scripts and compliance with procedures — how much of that is in the control of the worker? Yet it is considered a fundamental role of management — perhaps the most fundamental — to manage people.

Perhaps not surprisingly, managers react strongly when confronted with these ideas. Experience teaches that managers need to unlearn their current beliefs before they can accommodate what they would at first consider a 'radical' or even crazy alternative.

To help leaders unlearn, we help them study (try it). For example, they are invited to accompany a tradesman on his round and for every job that can't be completed on the first visit (usually more than 40% of them), they ask why. When they assemble their findings, we ask them to discuss the causes: how many are attributable to the tradesmen and how many to the system? Similarly, they may spend time listening to calls in a call centre. For every call, they pose the question: 'What caused this call to be longer or shorter?' When all the causes of variation have been identified, we ask them how many are attributable to the system and how many down to the worker.

The conclusion is invariably that it is the system that governs performance. As well as showing them the flaws in their current thinking (which condition the current design), taking part in exercises like this opens managers' eyes to the real opportunities for improvement.

Even having been confronted with the evidence, managers sometimes remain wedded to the view that it's all to do with people, naming 'poor performers' and recounting war stories of bad behaviour. It takes time to appreciate that the behaviour they are describing is a product of the system.

In my 2003 book[2], I described the questions managers should ask before deciding that they have a people problem. To abbreviate: Does the person know what to do? Do they have measures of achievement of purpose? Does the system support effective methods? Are there extrinsic forms of motivation (e.g. incentives) that drive behaviour? The point is this: it is only when all potential system causes of poor performance have been eliminated that can you be sure you have a problem with a person.

Yet the focus on people and 'performance management' is pervasive. The influential Francis Maude, the coalition's minister for the Cabinet Office, has adopted Jack Welch's 'rank and yank' approach to performance management[3]: all staff are performance-rated with a view to firing the bottom 10%; stupid and destructive, such a mechanism will inevitably cause people to cheat. Staff surveys, popular in the public sector, pinpoint symptoms, never causes. Culture change is probably the most absurd of all the ideas in the people management lexicon. People's behaviour is governed by the system, so when you change the system the culture changes (for free!)[4].

Friends and family test

The NHS has recently adopted the 'friends and family test'. It asks the question: would you recommend this hospital to your friends and family? I can't imagine wanting to recommend a hospital to anyone. The idea is faintly absurd: most people want a health service that solves their health problem. They are not looking for a great service experience as they might in leisure or retail services — they are seeking help and/ or a cure. In the private sector the friends and family test goes by the name of the 'Net Promoter Score' (NPS), and in this guise it has become popular over the last few years.

A small confession: even though NPS is completely useless in helping service organisations improve (see below), on our first assignment in a private-sector firm we say nothing about it, because we know the result of redesigning the system will be an immediate jump in the NPS score (usually from negative — 'customers hate us' — to positive — 'customers love us', striking when business plans call for improvement in percentage points from 'hate us' to 'don't like us much'); and because when it is reported to the board our work gets the directors' attention.

It makes it easier to help leaders see why NPS is a waste of time and money. First, it is what we call a 'lagging measure' — as with all customer-satisfaction measures, it assesses the result of something done in the past. Since it doesn't help anyone understand or improve performance in the present, it fails the test of a good measure — it can't help to understand or improve performance. But it is worse than that. The questions that follow on from, 'Would you recommend this service to a friend or family?', are all concerned with the behaviour of people delivering the service — in the NHS, nurses, doctors and auxiliary staff. But this is why it is attractive to conventional managers — since they believe it is the people who deliver services who should be the focus of management attention (the 5%), the test becomes an attractive device for controlling them.

Recently NPS changed its name from Net Promoter Score, to Net Promoter System. Systemic it is, but a systemic disease, not a source of systemic health and vitality.

It is possible to demonstrate the 95/5 principle by studying any system, even sales, which most people would probably consider the most individualistic of all the organisation's functions — after all, sales is all about the salespeople, isn't it? To show that it isn't, we made a video of a sales leader learning the truth[5].

Whistleblowing

The perspective that it's the system, not the people, and the way in which managers react to this counterintuitive truth, help us to understand why whistleblowers are treated in the way they are.

In his report on the failures at Mid Staffs, Francis recommended that to increase openness and transparency the current use of gagging clauses in the NHS should be banned. But he didn't explore why the NHS spends public money on gagging clauses in the first place. It is because the gaggees threatened to blow the whistle on the system, exposing the system conditions that produce the terrible consequences.

I have talked to a number of whistleblowers in the NHS. Most are motivated to act over matters of inadequate care or even unnecessary death. Whistleblowers point to the causes as being the way bureaucracy fills staff time, the lack, or inadequacy, of equipment or drugs, and the shortage of beds or space. These are all management (system) problems.

What's interesting is that managers rarely deny or argue about the substantive issue (patient neglect); for that they feign deep concern, paying lip-service to the facts and often sheltering behind vague mission-like mantras such as, 'we deliver world-class services'. They almost always mount an attack on the whistleblower. Whistleblowers are often criticised for using the 'wrong tone or language', including overblown terms like 'dangerous', and for procedural offences such as going over the heads of their managers. They are accused of having poor relations with other staff, fictitious complaints are sent to their professional body; they are accused of being bullies, frauds or even in some cases sex fiends. Sometimes managers ask security personnel to spy on whistleblowers to find grounds for hauling them over the coals. It seems anything will do, if it will turn the whistleblower into the problem.

It is because of the dissonance created. The real issues, for example, bed shortage, challenge managers' preoccupation with, in this case, reducing the number of beds. Managers can't cope with what is being said because of the implications (in their heads) for bed management. One whistleblower went public about a trust charging the taxpayer for operations that had already been paid for privately[6]. This is the way managers had found to get round the problem. They had to solve the problem to survive: make the budget.

This behaviour goes all the way to the top. Kay Sheldon, a board member of the Care Quality Commission (CQC), gave evidence to the House of Commons Health Select Committee about what happened to her when she disclosed cover-ups of incompetence by the regulator[7]. The CQC chair asked the Secretary of State to sack her and referred her without her knowledge for an assessment of her mental health. Whistleblowing is a dangerous endeavour.

Whistleblowers attract such shocking treatment because they blow the wrong whistle. If they informed on bad behaviour by staff they would be listened to. On the other hand, blowing the whistle on features of the system that challenge management's wrong-headed beliefs, and thereby also the status quo, brings down instant vilification.

It is the system that is the problem in healthcare and all other public services. When managers alter the system, they work on the 95%, which is why they get results they would never have put in a plan.

Chapter 16: Incentives always get you less

It is considered axiomatic that incentives drive performance: offering people rewards — pay for performance or payment for results — will cause them to do a better job. The uncomfortable truth is that while incentives *do* alter behaviour, it is not in the simplistic way economists expect. The reality is that rewards always get you less. If performance is incentivised, productivity falls. Although it is a truth well evidenced in psychological and behavioural research[1], it appears so outlandish to politicians and (conventional) managers that they ignore the dysfunctional consequences of rewards and punishments (carrots and sticks) that are to be seen are all around us.

In Chapter 15 I referred to a video featuring a leader of a financial sales organisation who discovered to her shock that it was the system that governed her sales figures, not the people. Studying her system revealed the behaviours that were being driven by the incentives in force.

To put it bluntly, to make their sales figures her people would cheat. Customers who rang in for something other than a purchase would be quickly passed on to someone else or put off, since there was no prospect of a sale. Agents would sell, or try to sell, customers products they didn't want or need — customers rarely took the hook and, as was obvious to anyone listening to the call, the impact on the customer relationship and the reputation of the firm was palpably awful. Even more striking (this was in the period of selling payment protection schemes), sales that didn't involve PPI were often not completed, since failing to meet a target ratio of payment protection policies to total sales meant the loss of all sales bonuses for the period. It turned out that the salespeople the boss considered the best (measured against targets) were in fact the least productive.

This is the first problem with incentives: they engage people's ingenuity in making the numbers, by fair means or foul. If you manage by attention to output, people do what they need to, to achieve the output you want: they cheat. This always happens when incentives are contingent — do this to get that. It focuses people's minds on how to 'get that', which is not at all the same as 'doing this', and is often at the expense of it. The reinforcement can either be positive (get the bonus — the carrot) or negative (avoid punishment — the stick).

I have already described the phenomenon of negative reinforcement (people focusing on meeting targets regardless of the impact on the system) in health, policing, local authorities and housing. If you are sat at the top of a hierarchy reading reports on targets achieved, like the leader described above, you will imagine your system is working, but you will have no knowledge of how much damage is being caused.

Consider what we have seen with the DWP's work programme. The 'doing this' (the purpose) is to help people get back into work. But the focus of suppliers is to 'get that', i.e. revenue. The result is 'parking' and 'creaming' — 'parking' is avoiding helping the neediest since they take more time and effort; 'creaming' is the opposite: focusing on those who are easiest to help and at the extreme claiming for people who have found a job on their own, without help from the provider. To get the payments, providers have resorted to paying job-seekers the minimum wage and lending them to employers for the period required to claim a result and make the target.

Elsewhere, providers have charged for tagging dead or non-existent offenders, while in social care people are moved on to personal budgets regardless of their suitability, and so on it goes. Payment by results gets you worse results[2].

Consequences like these are ubiquitous and systemic. Under pressure of incentives, and with no control over the system they work in, people willy-nilly channel ingenuity into falsifying outputs, hiding work and fudging reports. As a result, they become cynical and hostile towards management (and politicians), indifferent to other parts of their organisation or wider system with which they ought to cooperate, and bitter and disengaged from their work.

The second problem with incentives is that they halt innovation in its tracks (except that is in outwitting managers and finding new ways to cheat). Innovation requires people to think about their work and experiment with methods (hopefully) of doing it better. Incentive schemes based on activity targets effectively prevent that, as any 'stepping out of line' (doing what matters) is discouraged.

Cheating and choking off innovation are bad enough, but contingent incentives have an even darker side. They suck value out of the work, undermining pride and robbing workers of any sense of vocation. Under incentives the work is no longer intrinsically rewarding, because it has become a means to an end.

A number of psychological experiments have illustrated this phenomenon. Two groups are given the same task, one group incentivised, the other not. When a rest period is signalled, the incentivised group stops working while the non-incentivised group carries on. Other experiments have shown that incentivised groups do less work than non-incentivised groups. When children are rewarded with sweets for doing something they become less interested in the activity when the rewards cease (in one study the reward was for reading books — in effect the children were being taught not to value reading). If people are offered incentives to give blood, fewer do so than if they are not. When people are observed doing work, for example for the purposes of inspection, they lose interest in the task itself.

The findings are consistent: extrinsic motivational tools (carrots and sticks) sap intrinsic motivation. 'Do this to get that' devalues the 'this'. It explains the impact of incentives on public sector workers. No wonder public services are beset with high levels of turnover and low morale. People who to a large extent have chosen to work in the public sector for vocational reasons are being conditioned to believe that their activities are not worth doing for their own sake. Work is experienced as control and lack of autonomy, increasing stress and health-related problems[3].

Psychological studies show that the greater the desire for the carrot the more the dislike for the means required to get it; the passion for carrots is matched by a pathological distaste for working.

Much 'research' on incentives is composed of opinion studies among those using the schemes and argument about how to make them better (a sure sign they have problems). Research that questions the value of incentive schemes as such is much rarer. Thinktanks, often supported by political money, promote pay for performance irrespective of the evidence.

To go back to where I started, we have extensive experience of helping companies that have seen the light take out their sales incentive schemes. In every case sales go up! Would you believe it? Customer satisfaction also rises, which, in turn, has a further positive impact on sales. In these organisations there used to exist whole departments of people dedicated to dreaming up new wrinkles for their incentive schemes. They are no longer needed.

To take one of my favourite examples, most car dealers assume that without sales incentives they won't shift cars. One client has a number of dealerships in Canada. Studying revealed the tricks salespeople would use to make sales, in order to get the incentives, and the impact of the system on the customer. Today, all incentives have been removed. The dealerships offer prospective customers a brochure describing all the common industry sales tricks and promising that none apply here. Sales have gone up, and customer relationships improved — an important factor, since dealers rely on after-sales for the bulk of their business.

It is the same in any sales force. Incentives reduce cooperation between salespeople, lead to higher turnover (of customers too), and worsen the customer experience.

In the private sector, from time to time we come across organisations where all senior managers are incentivised. In one extreme example, individual incentive plans were kept under lock and key in the HR department and no one was allowed to see those of their peers. If you wanted to design a means of destroying the enterprise, you could hardly do better than that.

What *does* motivate people?

People motivate themselves. Research shows that high motivation demands three pre-conditions: autonomy, giving people control of the way they work; mastery, so that they are able to improve the work they do; and purpose, which is self-explanatory[4]. Intrinsic motivation — pride in work — is the engine of performance and, for that matter, health and wellbeing, too. It can't be emphasised enough that to generate innovation and improvement in public services we need a regime that is centred on these three conditions. I shall return to this in Chapter 28.

It is as Frederick Herzberg, the father of motivation theory, taught: if you want people to do a good job, give them a good job to do[5].

Part 4: Ideology, fashions and fads

Introduction

In Part 4 I shall take a look at some of the interventions driven by Whitehall in the name of reform, some ideological, some fashions and fads.

Ideological beliefs are grounded in economic theory. I shall begin this Part with the idea that people want choice in public services.

Fads and fashions usually erupt with a fanfare, enjoy a period of prominence, and then fade away to be supplanted by another. They are typically simple to understand, prescriptive, and falsely encouraging — promising more than they can deliver. Most importantly, fads and fashions are always based on a plausible idea that fits with politicians' and management's current theories and narratives — otherwise they wouldn't take off.

Given the thesis of this book, it won't surprise you that what follows is a negative critique. As we dig into the methods and theories of the fads and fashions, we discover their fundamental flaws and, where appropriate, I describe better methods grounded in evidence.

Chapter 17: Choice

Launching the Open Public Services White Paper in July 2011[1], David Cameron extolled the principle of choice. He claimed it wasn't just 'some theory' but a principle grounded in evidence. The only evidence he was able to cite was a study published by academics at the London School of Economics which purported to show that hospitals offering more choice had lower death rates.

In fact the evidence the prime minister relied on was roundly condemned in academic circles for being non-peer-reviewed and poor-quality research[2].

It is sad, almost pitiable, that a prime minister should grasp at this one straw to support an ideological view; one smidgen of so-called evidence in one public service to justify an agenda that will cover all public services. Tony Blair did something similar. In my 2008 book I described how he claimed that people who had been waiting for the NHS to fix them were pleased to have a 'choice' to go elsewhere to get their needs met[3]; equally desperate, equally myopic.

There is no evidence that people want choice in public services. When challenged, the ideological bloggers who assert the benefits and necessity of choice simply repeat the claims of the two prime ministers based on the same two paltry examples. I'm confident people simply want public services that work.

Ideologues claim that services will work better if providers feel the pressure of consumer choice. The best way to raise quality and value for money is competition, which is vital to give meaning to choice. Competition will cause providers to up their game.

It's an idea straight out of mainstream economic thinking — 'rational man' making choices in an efficient market, leading to competition that drives improvement. Neither rational man nor the efficiency of the market is a universal truth, and there is plenty of evidence to show it, but both are plausible. I shall return to economic theories and economists in Chapter 26.

The only 'game' that providers will certainly 'up' is their creativity in maximising their position. One example is supplying lowest-cost care services of fixed duration, which, as I described earlier (Chapter 10), takes the thermostat out of the system while maintaining revenue for the provider. In competitive tendering, a common tactic is for potential providers to bid low to win the contract in the knowledge that they can subsequently re-engineer the relationship to maximise additional income (more on this in Chapter 22). I have already described the gaming by which companies boost their revenues from outsourced offender-tagging and the work programme.

Cameron thinks choice will give patients the freedom to choose the healthcare they want. I don't know about you, but when I need specialist care I ask my GP who she would recommend; now that we have instilled the mantra of choice into healthcare we have to dance around the question, pretending that I must 'choose', but, thankfully, I still get her advice on whom to go to. I have neither the time nor inclination to research which specialist is 'best', and in any case official league tables almost always have validity issues.

Surveys show that 80% of people think that choice is a positive thing to have in public services. But this is like motherhood and apple pie — who wouldn't say that 'choice' is a good thing in reply to an open-ended question? But when asked to choose between statements a) 'make sure people who are ill get treatment quickly' and b) 'make sure people have a lot of choice about their treatment and care' (plus two others), a) wins hands down with 78% while b) gets 6%[4]. Although it is a question not asked by opinion-pollsters, it's a fair bet that most people want to get treatment as speedily as their condition requires. I know of many examples where people are happy to wait for a service that they know will work.

Politicians assume that choice will (for example) give social housing tenants more options about where they live. That's what Blair thought, and, because it had the word 'choice' in the title, he drove the widespread adoption of choice-based lettings, a wrong-headed adaptation of a Dutch scheme which created a massive citizen-unfriendly bureaucracy with other sub-optimal features. I described it in my last book[5]. Housing services that dropped choice-based lettings rid themselves of the costly bureaucracy and developed a service that gave prospective tenants a far better service which included choice over the things that really mattered to them.

The assumption is that the alternative to choice is people being obliged to take what they are given. But 'take-what-you-are-given' is a rhetorical device, a pre-emptive strike against dissent frequently employed by politicians in which any alternative to their policy is labelled as disastrous or foolhardy. But it is not the only alternative. Ironically, the way 'choice' has developed in services like drug treatment programmes is exactly that: you get what you are given because it is what the commissioner has 'chosen' to buy. In Chapter 10, I showed how the recent introduction of commissioning, essential to the choice agenda, has diminished people's control over how they experience services and led to the provision of services that don't meet people's needs. I have more to say on this in the following chapters on personal budgets and commissioning.

Despite abundant reports on the lack of evidence for choice[6] and ignoring the evidence pointing to its dysfunctional consequences, the government is enshrining the general right to choose in law[7].

The complement to choice in the government's strategy is 'diversity'. Diversity, Cameron said, was now the 'default' in public services: "Instead of having to justify why it makes sense to introduce competition...the state will have to justify why it makes sense to run a monopoly". By diversity he meant "...opening up public services to new providers and new ideas", likening public services to buying a mobile phone. I can't imagine Cameron has bought a mobile phone recently. It is a market that specialises in what is called 'confusion marketing', i.e. making claims that make comparisons more difficult, not less. It is also a market — like many others — where inertia rules, most customers remaining with the same provider unless irritation becomes too great to be ignored. Having said that, it is also true that the industry's marketing strategies have created a small number of 'churn junkies' — churn being industry-speak for customer turnover — who chase deals in the knowledge that threatening to leave will usually get them a better deal from the existing provider's 'saves team'.

Diversity is a euphemism for opening the door to private-sector suppliers. Cameron claimed the voluntary sector would benefit too, but in practice the policy of commissioning for scale ('bigger is better') does the opposite, squeezing out small-scale voluntary-sector providers, even highly-regarded existing ones[8].

Cameron insisted: "This white paper says loud and clear that it shouldn't matter if providers are from the state, private, or voluntary sector — as long as they offer a great service". Which no doubt would cause many people to wonder why it is that private-sector organisations with dreadful reputations for customer service are winning so much business in the public-sector marketplace.

What choice matters?

Politicians conflate two quite different issues when they talk about choice: the perceived benefit of lower costs through competition, and the intrinsic value for the recipient of having control over the service provided. The latter, as I illustrated in Chapter 10, is essential in developing services that work. And, paradoxically, it is the means for reducing costs. It is collaboration, not competition that drives costs down. Any pressure to reduce costs is a sure way to doom; it will drive costs up and worsen service.

This important distinction is evident in a report on choice by David Boyle, a Liberal-Democrat policy thinker, commissioned by the coalition government to research choice in public services[9]. Like many 'research' reports commissioned by politicians, Boyle's brief was not to question whether choice was a good thing, but instead to look into evidence about how it is implemented in practice. Politicians want research that tells them how to get more choice going, not to be told it's a bad idea.

Boyle and his Cabinet Office team decided to concentrate on schools, healthcare and social care, and set about meeting service users, professionals and interest groups from across the country to discover how people exercise choice in public services.

What he learned was that when asked what kind of choice they want, people don't talk of choices between providers (choice as competition) they talk of choices about the 'what and how' of services (choice as the intrinsic value of control). People want to choose in a whole range of areas where it is currently impossible: for example, to go to bed when they want to rather than at the time of the carer visit; to spend personal budgets as they choose, not according to an official list; to get their specific, personal needs met through services which operate in silos.

Boyle argued that if there is a place for choice it is in driving up quality, not driving down price. He was right: improving quality reduces costs. In Boyle's language, people want more 'authority' to ensure their specific needs can be accommodated. They need information about all the possible ways of meeting their needs, not just the services that are officially sanctioned. Some people want face-to-face advice. In short, people want flexibility — they want services to start from where they are, rather than, in Boyle's words, "where the theorists think they should be".

Boyle's report provides further evidence for the approach I described in Chapter 10. He can see that the flexibility at the core of the approach 'could potentially release huge resources'. I would only argue about the word 'potentially', the release of resources being a given.

The irony is that people's experience of services is precisely what Cameron described as the dreadful alternative: they get the package dreamed up by commissioners and providers, not the one that they want or need. In his speech launching the White Paper, Cameron declared: 'The old narrow, closed, state monopoly is dead'. Yet we have 'narrow' (specialised) services that don't match needs because they are standardised through competition on price. This may not be monopolistic but it is certainly state-controlled in the broadest sense. Note that this is not an argument about whether services should be provided by the state or the private sector — it is an argument about what good services look like.

And good services in the public sector feature collaboration, not competition.

Chapter 18: Personal Budgets

The first time I heard the phrase 'doomed to succeed' it was being used by officials in local-authority care services to describe personal budgets. Personal budgets (PB) for care were dreamed up by the last Labour government. They ticked two of the government's boxes: they represented 'choice', and more sneakily shifted responsibility (and cost) for administering care provision to the individual. Ironically, the means by which care and support recipients were moved to the PB regime was targets (choice up to a point, then). The high volume of take-up is taken to represent the efficacy and desirability of the policy; and any research focuses on improving PB use, not on whether or not they work[1]. But it isn't hard to read between the lines.

I have to start by saying that personal budgets do work for some, but even where they do, they necessarily involve sub-optimisation. Where PB doesn't work the sub-optimisation is considerably worse.

To start with the general sub-optimisation, it takes the form of administrative bureaucracy. The starting-place for getting a PB is assessment, in the shape of either self-assessment, 'supported' self-assessment or assessment by an expert. Whichever route is taken, assessment means forms to fill in and here we immediately hit the larger form of sub-optimisation: questions on forms don't always take account of the variety of people's strengths, needs and circumstances.

But staying for the moment with administration, in many local authorities the assessment has to be input into a computer system, usually one that wasn't designed for the purpose. The system produces an 'indicative' budget (the money that is likely to be allocated), which is then typically adjusted to take into account budget limits, the amount of carer support, the inadequacy of the forms in articulating needs or eligibility and severity of need. The PB has to be 'signed off' by an approval panel, usually with a hierarchy of signing authorities, dependent on the size of the award. As well as the needs assessment, there is also a requirement for a 'risk assessment' (more on risk in Chapter 23).

Assessment of need and risk is followed by a financial assessment, where the 'contribution' (it was originally called a 'charge') the recipient will need to make is determined. This can be confusing and absorbs further time and resource. Some claimants give up at that point when they discover that their contribution represents the bulk of the cost.

If you are like me, you might have noticed that none of this does anything for the person who needs help. The period from assessment to 'ready-to-go' can be lengthy and difficult. This is the sub-optimisation that applies to all, and from here we see more of the flaw that drives sub-optimisation for the many: a lack of flexibility. People's needs frequently vary or fluctuate, so we hit the barrier I described in Chapter 10; anything that standardises a service or breaks it up into separate specialisms thereby prevents it from absorbing the variety of demand.

Typically an award ties 'pots' of money to different aspects of PB users' needs; for example, personal care, social support, transport or mobility all have their own allocations. Often PB users find themselves obliged to challenge the allocations, frequently needing an advocate to do so. The extent of the obligation to use money only for its specified purpose varies around the country.

In allocating needs to budgets confusion arises in matching the two — for example is heating an agoraphobic's home classified as coming from the 'heating' pot or the 'disability' pot? Let me give you an example of the madness: Bob (not his real name) returned home in a wheelchair having lost the use of both legs. His house had been prepared for him with improved access, grab rails and a stair lift, but Bob soon found his biggest problem was using the kitchen. The local authority considered adapting Bob's kitchen or helping Bob move house; they had budgets for both. While the machinations went on Bob found his own solution: a pump-up cushion which would take him to the height he wanted when he used the kitchen. The local authority was stumped; they didn't have a budget for that.

To go back to the assessment phase: some potential users not totally put off by the size of their contribution change their mind when they realise that what amounts to a small grant will be closely managed. This is not unlike tax credits, where people on credits give up using them because the hassle outweighs the value. Some potential PB users feel that their families are being penalised for acting as carers as this 'adjustment' reduces the award.

The administration required is not insubstantial. If a PB includes employing people, the recruitment and payroll has to be done. Making arrangements for services and paying for them also becomes the responsibility of the PB user. If the recipient can't or is unwilling to take on the administration, they can pay a 'support provider' to do it, taking funds from their award (further reducing the value of choice). There is now a market for support providers, a non-value adding activity.

The PB can be in the control of the user, or the local authority will service the PB using the fund to commission and pay for services, or a third-party support organisation may be employed by the PB user to administer these things. These alternatives are described as 'deployment options', a further example of valueless choice.

PB schemes differ in their adherence to rules on how the award can be spent. In some cases any spend on 'exceptions' has to be referred for a decision. PB users can find themselves with excess funds at the end of a period (a sure sign of a problem fitting allocations to needs), and this too has to be referred to the supervising/assessment team.

Any PB requires regular reviews and, if necessary, re-assessments. On top of those, they have to be monitored by the local authority and audited on a regular basis. The audit process requires the completion of more forms and requires that PB users keep records.

When it comes to purchasing services, another set of problems raises its head. Being commissioned by the local authority not the user, sometimes the services don't fit needs (as I described in Chapter 10). Often the supply of services doesn't adapt to changing needs (I called this removing the thermostat). PB users experience problems with the continuity of care personnel and often find it difficult to recruit help for short durations. Sometimes PB users won't attend drop-in or day-care centres because they have to pay. When such collective activities don't exist, it becomes the PB users' responsibility to 'pool their purchasing power', in local-authority-speak, to get them organised. As if.

PB users often become anxious about whether the services they want to buy are within the terms of their PB or require 'permission', so they may seek guidance. They worry when they hear that their case is 'closed', compounding the uncertainty induced by the lack of continuity in relationships throughout the process.

Given all these problems and uncertainties, it is no surprise that a mini-industry has grown up devoted to providing guidance on the administration of PBs. All because of the simple truth that in any system rules will fail to take account of variety.

So yes, PBs can work sometimes, and they will certainly be seen to work by those who want to extol their virtue — but at what cost?

Let's return to what we know about effective service provision. It requires a thorough understanding of the person, both strengths and needs; it needs knowledge of their context; it has to put the recipient at the centre of defining what a good life (or good death) means to him or her; it has to have continuity in the relationship, and it needs to be thermostatic, capable of responding to fluctuations in need. Finally, the default position is that it should lead to the 're-enabling' of the person to lead their own life[2].

'Personal budgets' are not the most effective way of achieving those aims. As we have seen, for all but the canniest of users — i.e. those who have least need of them — PBs are a poor bargain. It is not beyond the wit of man to design a system that meets individual needs with the minimum of administration and at lower overall cost.

I know many public-sector commentators and practitioners might interpret what I have described as effective service provision as 'co-production'. It could be. I put it that way because co-production, an initiative that began with identifying problems associated with taking police officers off the beat and into vehicles, has problems of operational definition — what it means in concrete terms — and, from there, what do you actually do?[3].

Chapter 19: Commissioning

I shall focus here on commissioning for care and support services; commissioning for outsourced services like procurement and housing repairs will be tackled in the chapter on procurement (Chapter 23).

I have already described the essential problems with commissioning in Chapter 10, but to recap:

Despite the rhetoric from Whitehall about commissioning personalised services, in practice commissioners focus on price, even priding themselves on price cuts negotiated with suppliers. If a service is commissioned on price, it has to have a specification, otherwise it can't be priced by competing suppliers. If a service is specified, by definition it is also standardised. Again by definition, a standardised service will fail to meet the variety of demands. So commissioning as practised will necessarily result in under- or over-provision for many service users, generating supplementary (failure) demand. So costs will go up. One more time: if you manage cost, costs rise.

Now let's review what we know about successful service provision in what I have been calling 'my-life-has-fallen-off-the-rails' services.

Effective service provision requires a thorough understanding of the individual person, both their strengths and their needs, in their life context. It puts the recipient at the centre, allowing them to define what a good life (or good death, as the case may be) means to them. There must be continuity in the relationship, and it needs to be 'thermostatic', sensitive to fluctuations in need. The default goal is 're-enablement', that is, putting individuals back in control of their own lives.

Successful commissioning means finding providers who can do these things. Many initially may not have all the capabilities required, but that is of secondary significance since the practical elements can be taught. The first and most important selection criterion is attitude. Does the organisation have, firstly, the right attitude about care and support for the vulnerable? Secondly, does it show the preparedness to work collaboratively with the commissioner to develop measures and methods to achieve the purpose?

With respect to the latter, commissioners should be capable of helping providers develop measures that make people's needs, strengths, context and ambitions concrete, such that they can be measured. These measures will be used to track progress over time. The crucial point here is that the measures used to track what happens to individuals or families *are the same as those reported to commissioners*, no more, no less. The current practice of aggregating data has no value and should be abandoned.

Commissioners should foster and be involved in experimenting with service provision, encouraging providers to work to these principles: that the recipient of the service defines the outcome sought and only the expertise required is 'pulled' into the relationship. To this effect commissioners should spend the bulk of their time in the work, alongside providers.

Examples of effective care services illustrate what being effective takes and the implications for commissioning:

Person-centred services: people with learning difficulties

When staff at Community Lives Consortium (CLC), a Welsh social enterprise which provides support to people with learning difficulties, studied their service, they discovered that their priorities were effectively determined by the commissioning local authority's standardised assessment process, based on completion of a 21-page core assessment form. Structuring the work around the form prevented CLC staff listening and responding to their users' real needs. With better demand information, CLC could engage constructively with commissioners to find more effective ways of responding to user needs. Revised measures reflecting users' desired outcomes fed into new, personalised service delivery plans that were individually developed with the people the organisation was supporting. One effect of these improvements was to eliminate substantial amounts of waste arising from rework and process-checking — administration that was previously carried out separately now could be undertaken as part of their daily support activities with users[1].

Person-centred services: people with health and care needs

Studying the health and social care system across a community in Gloucester revealed that 5% of the users consumed 50% of the overall resource; 86% of demand presenting to services was failure demand; and that 25% of staff time was devoted to value work. Essentially it took 400 hours of work to produce 100 hours of value.

Using 'difficult' cases (i.e. that the system was having trouble coping with), two teams comprising nurses, social workers, physiotherapists and occupational therapists started to learn how to use new principles to understand and support people in need. Although taking demand from a medical part of the system (via the GP), 90% of people they met were in need of more general support, 53% exclusively so and two-thirds predominantly.

Skills (rather than jobs, roles or remits) were deployed as required, and support and care work was designed around the specific things that people actually needed. This revealed that the key skills required to help understand and rebalance people were predominantly not clinical or technical but effective interpersonal (especially listening), organisational and problem-solving skills. Technical competences obviously remained important for 'fix me' (medical) demands, but it was paying attention to *social* needs ('help me' demands) that evidently had most effect in securing better outcomes for both the individual and the system as a whole.

The new system based on end-to-end flow is radically different from the previous model. It is radically simpler too, demonstrating that much of the complexity and need for co-ordination in today's arrangements is designed in: it exists as a feature of today's system of provision, not as a feature inherent in today's demand. The ratio of value to waste work has moved to 80:20[2].

Somerset has developed a very similar model, building local teams around GP practices. The first study of 120 people consistently showed prevention of hospital admissions, reduced lengths of stay, reduced social care support and prevention of long-term residential placements.

Reduction of strain and prevention of carer breakdowns was another notable outcome. A wider cohort study has since shown significantly better outcomes for 30-day re-admissions and social care costs after the intervention — effectively breaking the cycle of growing dependency and decline[3].

Built into this way of working is the anticipation that services will flex and change over time according to recipients' needs. Some people's requirements will grow, others lessen, still others will change in nature. Commissioners should focus on the nature of demand (in terms of 'people-with-need', not, as is currently the practice, in terms of the off-the-peg packages provided), tracking changes in kind and volumes, which should be expected to fall.

Commissioning in this way will be to commission on cost — paying for what is provided — not price; as ambitions are realised and needs are met, costs will fall.

Chapter 20: Managing demand

At the time of writing, 'managing demand' is the latest fad to have hit public services. It purports to respond to the austerity agenda: 'Rising demand, changing demographics and increasingly stretched finances mean that the choice for local authorities and public service providers is stark: change the way they work, or face the possibility of service retrenchment, increasing irrelevance and perpetual crisis management', according to a report announcing the idea[1].

Demand management fits the current narrative. It assumes a world where demand is fated to outstrip supply and could overwhelm services entirely if action isn't taken. In other words, there is a sword of Damocles hanging over our heads. This of course is entirely false. The problem is not one of demand rising; it is that demand is being amplified by the ways in which we design and manage services. But the narrative of doom creates a burning platform for the gullible to be exploited.

Managing demand is apparently an 'emerging science'. According to the report, there are five types of demand: failure demand, avoidable contact, excess demand, preventable demand and co-dependent demand. If this is a science, it fails at the first fence: none of these types of demand (including failure demand, which *I* have defined clearly) has a useful operational definition, that is to say what each means in concrete terms, so that you would know it if you saw it. At one point excess demand is defined as 'demand beyond that which could be considered genuine' and it is suggested that avoidable demand 'arises where bad behaviours or relationships are created or reinforced by patterns of service delivery'. But what do these things mean?

I am confident that the primary influence on the concept of managing demand is our own work on the subject of demand. In the latter period of the last Labour government a civil servant in the Cabinet Office became enthusiastic about the idea of failure demand. It is an easy idea to understand (it's a major cost) and (if you think about it that way, as she did) also to misunderstand. The civil servant mandated local authorities to audit their services for volumes of failure demand, report them to Whitehall, and then set targets for reducing it. Given that targets are themselves a major cause of failure demand in services, this is a nonsense. Councils were given no operational definition (she could have used mine), sending people into a spin about what to count as failure, and, as with any target, the game began: how to minimise the volumes reported.

Practitioners of our methods in local authorities voiced concern. Whitehall was dabbling in something it hadn't understood. My sources told me that fed up with hearing the words 'Seddon' and 'Vanguard', the civil servant in charge changed the name from failure demand to 'avoidable contact'. Immediately the press accused the government of trying to 'avoid' providing services[2].

I bumped into the official at a conference and suggested the people raising objections should be listened to. Her reply was that she could muster as large a group that supported her initiative. I said, "I think it was Socrates who said you can't find the truth by counting heads". She replied, "You don't need to tell me that, I'm a classics scholar".

But back to operational definitions: is failure demand the same as avoidable contact? And what do excess, preventable and co-dependent demand mean in concrete terms? The only clues are in the few examples and suggestions cited in the report, but interpreting them isn't easy as most of them are not specifically tied to the five demand types.

We could start with the two that have definitions, even though they are not concrete. Some people litter their streets. This is labelled as an example of both 'excess' and 'avoidable' demand. An experiment was conducted. Streets were cleaned on only one side. The idea was to demonstrate the scale of the problem to local people. The un-cleaned side of the street was photographed and videoed. Some participating councils organised a community clean up after the 48-hour experiment and posted the photographs and videos on their web sites alongside information about the cost of street cleaning, with links to their budget pages.

Did it work? We aren't told. Compare this to what Portsmouth City Council learned. Providing an outstanding repairs and maintenance service to social housing tenants had a wholly unexpected consequence: people took greater responsibility for keeping their environment clean[3].

The report suggests other ways of managing excess demand: charging (to act as a deterrent) for services like bulky collections; introducing fines for 'non-compliance' like littering and failing to sort household waste; and changing eligibility criteria for care services. Many councils already charge for bulky collections. In some cases making it difficult for people to dispose of things increases fly-tipping. Penalties are likely to cause similar dysfunctional side effects. They do nothing to help councils understand and act on causes of problems, assuming that blame must lie with the citizen. Rationing care services has the reliable effect of raising costs.

Another cited example of excess demand is 'the state providing more than is needed'. This is clearly excess provisioning, in demand terms the mismatch of demand and supply caused by the way services are commissioned (Chapter 19). It is a large problem caused by the design of the system itself.

'Preventable' demand is confusing, signifying two different things. If it is demand that presents a second time because it wasn't addressed at a previous point of contact (as is common in care services), it is failure demand. If on the other hand it is (say) obesity, we should be describing obesity demand as a measure used to assess the effectiveness of experiments, to learn if in fact it is preventable.

We're not much clearer about what the authors mean by 'co-dependent demand', other than that provided by the question: 'to what extent is demand unintentionally reinforced by service dependence?' The answer is quite a lot, through personal budgets, commissioning and outsourcing, but this is a provisioning not a demand problem.

The protagonists approve the fashionable concept of 'nudge' (see next chapter), but provide only one example. Having assessed the failure demand occurring as a result of certain letters sent out to residents, a council redesigned the letters to make them more understandable.

But this is hardly a 'nudge', being rather a simple exercise in cutting failure demand by doing what should have been done in the first place, drafting letters that people can understand.

When we turn to what the authors call the steps for system change, we learn that the short-term strategy should be eliminating excess demand, while redesigning services, followed by early intervention, prevention and resilience, should form the medium- and long-term focus respectively.

But what we know about eliminating demand in care and support services is that it squeezes the balloon, making it appear in a different form somewhere else. People want and need services that work from their point of view. Telling them to go away simply stores up greater costs for the future, no matter how it's done.

If the short-term strategy is itself manufacturing failure demand, a medium-term redesign will be a recipe for producing it faster, amplifying demand systemically.

Further, the distinction between the medium-term and long-term strategies is false. It draws the usual distinction between reactive and proactive/preventative services. However, effective public services eliminate the distinction. For example, studying organised crime shows that the son of the criminal father becomes a criminal father in his turn, and the cycle repeats. An effective reactive intervention into that cycle is also a successful proactive intervention for future generations. The common distinction between reactive and proactive is really just a manifestation of the current failure to see people and communities in context and over time. It treats the demands placed by each individual as separate from those placed by any other individual and as separate from those placed by the same individual earlier in time or through a different agency.

In short, the authors of the report think that providing effective services which meet their purpose from a citizen's point of view is the *final* thing to do (the "long term" strategy), whereas in fact it is the *only* thing to do. No one applies for a service saying, "please manage my demand", they do it saying, "please create value for me". Demand management is just another example of the thinking that characterises today's public services — 'keep them out or get them out' (otherwise we'll fall over). What we ought to be doing is 'help them out' (as I illustrate in Chapter 10).

The necessary order for improvement is *effective* then *efficient* then *sustainable*. Managing demand reverses this order. Focusing on sustainability first leads to rationing. Focusing on efficiency before effectiveness leads to faster failure. We will never get to effective because management will be tied up in further crises dealing with the consequences of the first two approaches, which fit with its current narrative. The fundamental logic at work in demand management is to treat demand, and therefore citizens, as the problem. The real problem is the way we have designed and managed services.

As the authors admit, the evidence for this "emerging science is nascent" — I would say non-existent or at least spurious in the extreme. Its embryonic state does not prevent them going on to produce an incredible financial projection: managing demand will apparently generate savings of almost £3bn.

Managing demand is just a collection of ideas and initiatives, some good, some bad, about what to do about demand. There is nothing wrong with experimenting, as many of the examples show, but the illustrations provided do not amount to a coherent theory. The protagonists of the emerging science are right that the needs people have don't match the way service is designed and delivered, so the very basis of those services needs to be challenged — but the way to do that is not to manage demand, it is to *understand* it.

To go back to the beginning: from our years of experience, there are only two types of demand that need to be thoroughly understood). They are failure demand (*demand caused by a failure to do something or so something right for the customer*) and value demand (*the demand the service exists to serve*). Unmet value demands are best understood as just that: value demands we don't currently service, but maybe should. There are plenty of those in both public and private sectors.

Chapter 21: Nudge

'Nudge' theory got coalition ministers so excited that a 'Nudge Unit' (as the Behavioural Insights Team is usually called) was set up in the Cabinet Office to apply "insights from academic research in behavioural economics and psychology to public policy and services".

Given that I'm an organisational psychologist, you might think that I'd support such a move. And I did, briefly. But in this chapter I'm going to use 'Nudge', chips and salad to explain why theory and knowledge matter so much to the business of delivering better public services — and just how wrong Whitehall can get it.

Perhaps the appeal of 'Nudge' was the promise of getting something done about 'them', the people out there, whose behaviour needs to change. Perhaps it was that the authors of the book that expounded 'Nudge' to the world, and started the whole bandwagon rolling, Richard Thaler and Cass Sunstein, were advisers to President Obama. Or perhaps it was that 'Nudge' offered a neat pseudotheory — a cover for Whitehall to try and push through any amount of 'here's one I prepared earlier' ideas, pet projects and prejudices. Incidentally, I wonder how many ministers read the book[1].

Whatever its appeal, those are my objections to 'Nudge'. It takes good science and experimentation, wraps it up in a sow's ear of incoherent and misunderstood theory, and invites politicians with a quite different agenda to apply the theory in a wholly different context (UK public services are not US supermarkets).

Chips and salad

It is telling that, having come up with a thesis they think will solve many of the world's problems, the authors of the book-of-the-thesis begin the book with a made-up example.

That's how it is with 'Nudge'. The authors tell an elaborate and therefore all the more convincing story about taking ideas developed in supermarkets and applying them to school dinners. They describe experiments run in dozens of American schools to display the food in such a manner that pupils were nudged to make better choices. To cut a long story short, they put the salad at the front and the chips at the back. But, by their own admission, they never did these experiments. So we don't know the results. But I've known toddlers who can reach past a mountain of green food to get at the bad stuff — never mind school kids.

This chips-and-salad fairy tale is used to establish the basic principle of nudging: libertarian paternalism. People remain free to do what they like but we try to influence them, to steer their choices, through what Thaler and Sunstein call "choice architecture" (where we put the chips). Libertarian paternalism, we are told, is "relatively weak, soft and non-intrusive" and choices are not "blocked, fenced off, or significantly burdened". Now most of us would probably agree that non-intrusive nudging is a better way to run a country than the indiscriminate use of torture and nerve gas. But if we're going to create a theory of choice architecture and define it this carefully — let's stick to the definition.

If, like me, you are forgiving of the fiction and want to see what 'Nudge' has to offer about eating more healthily, you read on. And this is what you discover. Obesity is a major problem. There is lots of data about its extent and consequences, all confirming the view that current choices can't be the best means of promoting wellbeing. Large plates encourage more eating; if your friends are fat you are more likely to become fat too; fat people tend to have fat friends; when we eat with other people we eat more. So the implicit advice on tackling obesity would seem to be to eat off smaller plates, choose thin friends and eat alone.

The authors are American. America has a significant problem with obesity (and the UK is catching up). For many poor families it is cheaper to eat fast food than buy ingredients and cook. Why is fast food so cheap? Because meat is mass-produced in unpleasant factory conditions[2]. Moreover, the feedstuff is primarily heavily subsidised grain[3]. Perhaps the authors simply chose the wrong fiction for their example. But it's already becoming clear that the main problem is not fat, greedy people but a *system* that enables — even fosters — obesity. A chips-and-salad nudge won't do much to change the incidence of obesity in America. But government could act coherently to change the system.

America also has a significant problem with management fads — from Business reengineering to Benchmarking to Six Sigma to... 'Nudge' (and the UK is catching up).To the extent that there is meat behind the 'Nudge' thesis it is sound research in social psychology, but many of the research findings don't actually represent nudges as defined by Thaler and Sunstein. This matters because, currently, everything that can be passed off as a nudge will be. And, as we have already seen, when bad theory with no evidence behind it gets smuggled into government policy-making, it's we, the citizens, who suffer. So let's take a look at some of the ways that good research has been hijacked by 'Nudge' theory.

Hijacked

For example, human behaviour is often subject to inertia (social psychologists call it the 'status quo bias'). The 'Nudge' authors describe how it can be harnessed by designing default options. Default options influence people's behaviour with regard to, for example, joining pension plans or signing up for magazine subscription (sellers know that many people won't bother to cancel in the cancellation period). But are these examples nudges? Rather than putting salad in front and chips at the back, they're putting out salad *instead of* chips.

Another example from social psychology is herd behaviour. Groups influence behaviour. They develop their own norms and standards and put peer pressure on group members. We have a desire to conform, so we tend to 'follow the herd'. Many of the social psychology studies are, in fact, concerned with dysfunctional examples of the phenomenon, such as market bubbles, football riots, or looting. Anyway, herding doesn't fit with the authors' definition of nudge. Changing behaviour by encouraging the herd to vilify those who don't want to change is probably unethical and using social coercion is more like bullying than "relatively weak, soft and non-intrusive" nudging. Rather than putting salad in front and chips at the back, they're getting your friends to send you to sit on your own if you choose the chips.

Another example is 'anchoring'. It describes the way people are influenced by the first piece of information offered — so if you are selling something, start with a high price and the final price will appear more like a bargain. ("Not five pounds, madam, not four pounds, not even three pounds sir, I'm asking just two pounds...") But 'anchoring' is not a nudge. Rather than putting salad in front and chips at the back, they're putting out bowls of old, limp salad in order to make the final bowl of crispy leaves look more appealing.

Or take what is called 'availability bias' — the tendency to overestimate the probability of events associated with memorable occurrences. Thus, when a plane crashes we think plane crashes are more probable. The authors cite examples of how information can bias people's judgements. We saw a version of this phenomenon when, in the era of David Blunkett as Home Secretary, citizens were asked if they feared crime. Asking the question increased fear. In the same way, social workers and police officers tend to have a negative view of society because they see more of its problems. Rather than putting salad in front and chips at the back, they're showing people in the lunch queue a video of someone choking to death on chips.

My point is that the psychology literature teaches the value of learning through experimentation. What matters is to learn which interventions help to meet demand or to do the job that public services are meant to be doing. Ones that do should be used. Ones that don't should be dropped.

To develop knowledge we have theories, which we define carefully, and then we test them. Confirmation or dis-conformation lead to knowledge (the ability to predict). 'Nudge' fails doubly in this regard. First, to have value, 'Nudge' should have been an appeal to learn from experimentation, taking pointers and ideas from the subject literature. But it was presented as a general theory of everything, with a lack of adherence to the operational definition, so almost anything can be a nudge. This won't help us learn, but it will create a bandwagon effect among those who are less than critical. Second, as I explain in Chapter 26, 'Nudge' theorists also choose to ignore social psychological research that doesn't suit their narrative. To echo the critique of economics in that chapter, we can reasonable say that 'Nudge' theory "has no principled discrimination about what constitutes just and proper argumentation within its own sphere".

Mis-applied

And so 'Nudge' set off on its own primrose path. Suddenly everything is a nudge: painting lines on roads, removing lines on roads, putting sound clicks into devices like phones to give users feedback, legislation for employers to have insurance schemes, sending out pamphlets to encourage recycling — even changing the clocks in spring is, apparently, a nudge for us to get up an hour earlier. Some of what's called a nudge is mistake-proofing: for example, you have to remove your card from an ATM before it will release your money. (You can't go and sit down unless you've put the salad on your tray.)

And Whitehall is dutifully trudging down the path. George Osborne decided a good nudge would be to submit customers to a two-week cooling-off period after signing up for a retail store card. The retailers lobbied against it; I'm confident it would have narked customers if it had become law. Then the government announced in its mid-term review that perceived store-card issues would be tackled by retailers agreeing to a 'good practice' training scheme and a seven-day ban on incentives for new card-holders, while legislation would empower the regulator to control the cost and duration of credit. No nudge here. Rather than putting salad in front and chips at the back, Osborne first tried to fence off the chips and then passed a chip law.

The Nudge Unit was reported to have drawn up a survey called "signature strengths" which was mandatory for job seekers — if they didn't complete the test they were told they might be at risk of losing benefits. No nudge here, then; take the salad or else. But those taking the test discovered that the same positive results — "your strengths" — were given, regardless of the answers jobseekers gave to the questions. The test was described as "scientifically shown to identify people's strengths" but in truth it was a bogus psychometric test used to attempt to nudge the unemployed using sham science[4].

Recent legislation giving employees the right to ask for flexible hours is described as a nudge for employers. Really? You can ask a dinner-lady for salad.

And families are being nudged to take on personalised budgets for special-needs school transport. You can go to the kitchen and prepare your own salad. Our own work shows that substantial amounts of money are wasted on special-needs transport; moving people to personalised budgets may fit the government's agenda, but whether nudge or not, the result will be to increase the waste.

This is not to deny that the Nudge Unit carried out some potentially useful experiments — for example, using text messages to encourage payment of fines and opting out rather than opting in to foster organ donation. But these are more properly conceptualised as experiments, not nudges. The chips are out of sight; these are experiments in making the salad more attractive. And we might reflect on why people in public services are not experimenting (surely it is them that should?) and that it takes a 'Nudge Unit' to do so.

Flushed with enthusiasm, the Cabinet Office decided to cash in on the Nudge Unit by putting it up for sale. Alas, there were no takers, so it was passed on to Nesta instead[5]. I'm not surprised no one was killed in the rush to buy a bunch of people conducting experiments. We can all do that, and indeed we should. It is essential for the development of public policy; in fact, as I shall argue in Chapter 29, policy should be thought of as an opportunity to experiment.

But 'Nudge' is a fashion; like all such fashions, it will wane. Beware the next fad and those who come bearing it, and insist on policy that experiments, identifies what works and applies it rigorously — rather than policy that pushes through prejudices and preconceptions.

Chapter 22: Procurement –
How to ensure you don't get what you want

Imagine you are a public-sector leader. There's something you want to do to improve your service, and you know who you want to help you. Perhaps you have used this person or group before; perhaps they have worked for a colleague. Either way, you know they are good at what they do, and you want some of it, too. You might think you should call them up to talk about what you need and work out how to do it.

Well, you can't. Regulation has seen to that.

If you want to buy anything in the public sector, the first thing you will have to do is describe your requirement in broad terms and send it out as a request for service. Any interested party that responds to your request must complete a pre-qualification questionnaire, giving details about their business. Then a panel must be formed, which is there to ensure the selection of the supplier is done objectively, usually including a 'procurement professional'. Then, a more detailed specification (the request for proposal, RFP) needs to be written and sent out to the organisations that have expressed an interest and completed the pre-qualification questionnaire.

Next, the organisations tendering must submit a detailed response to your RFP. If they have questions about your requirements, you must make those questions and your answers available to all the other organisations bidding. You can, if you wish, choose to do this by holding open meetings with all the interested parties. What you cannot do is hold private meetings with any of them.

When the due date for tender submission is reached, you convene the panel, which will make 'objective' judgements about the bids against a set of criteria of its devising. The judgements are expressed in points, and the bidder that receives the highest number will be awarded the contract. The odds are high that it will not be the organisation you wanted.

At this point, like many others, you may just give up and forget about getting help altogether. All that effort, for all parties, most of whom you would never have wanted to use anyway. What a waste.

This is called professional procurement, and it is a disease. Let's look at where it goes awry.

The buying process is inherently weighted in favour of large firms. One reason is that it involves a great deal of administration for which small firms have neither the time nor the resources. They are also favoured by the scoring of the pre-qualification questionnaire. Points are awarded for size (bigger is better), audited accounts, registration to ISO 9000 (wrongly assumed to be a mark of quality) and references, while copious documentation will also be required on 'account management structure' (how you invoice for work), business continuity policy, environmental policy, equality of opportunity policy, ethical trading code of practice ('we don't employ slaves or children'), health and safety policy, corporate liability insurance, training policy and, often, more.

Clearly it will make sense for resource-rich organisations to draw up pre-prepared documentation to satisfy foreseeable requirements, while small organisations will feel obliged to write what they see to be a load of unnecessary nonsense. As one industry insider put it: "The big boys have an army of spin doctors who know all the tricks, can tick the right boxes and convince the buyer they only care about the customer without getting caught lying". While the 'big boys' have salespeople out winning contracts, small suppliers have to attend to it themselves. Not having time for spin, they are more likely to have the disadvantage of being honest.

You might say to yourself that putting down on paper what you need is tiresome but rational. But given that you are seeking help from someone who has expertise you don't, writing it down becomes a constraint on what might be achieved which can only be altered by a cumbersome process involving all the parties. If a potential supplier has the temerity to submit a proposal along the lines of 'what you ask for is not what you need and you should do this instead', it won't get past the panel because it won't score points on their 'objective' criteria.

Part of your specification will include the requirement for suppliers to quote costs. In many circumstances the costs of providing support cannot be known, so bidders can only be encouraged to bid high. On the other hand, in some circumstances exactly the same service is provided to other customers and industry bid costs are well known. In those circumstances, to win business some tenderers will bid very low ('suicide bids' in the trade), since price is heavily weighted in the scoring. In some cases (for example the procurement of supplies) there are so many items that it is impractical to quote for the costs of all so a sample is chosen, providing a lucrative loophole for the successful bidder to wriggle through (see later).

When, to your dismay, your preferred supplier fails to win despite scoring high marks on evidence of being able to deliver (the reason you wanted the outfit in the first place) it may be because it was marked down for failing to list the people who will be involved in delivery (small companies can't commit people ahead of winning work), insufficient policy documentation, not being registered to ISO 9000, and so on. You may plead for what you want, but the 'we must be objective' machine will grind on and ignore you.

The process can take a considerable time. I have known it to take more than a year; much longer than it would to provide the service.

As you will have gathered, Vanguard consultants have considerable experience in housing repairs. I shall use this service to illustrate how the procurement process works across the whole of the public sector.

The modern thinking among procurement professionals is that bigger is better. Smaller contractors increasingly fall foul of the Whitehall-driven belief that having one large-scale supplier will achieve economies of scale while also streamlining the contracting process and reducing the risks associated with it. As I shall show, this is false.

Small contractors are thought to be 'unsophisticated'. They generally can't point to KPIs (i.e. targets) or a hierarchy devoted to 'management information'. That is perfectly true. But then these features are not a sign of sophistication, rather a warning signal of poor performance to come.

When tenderers offer 'suicide bids', they do so in the knowledge that they have ways of 'fixing' the revenue issue. In housing repairs, the loophole is 'supply of materials'. In this service, as in outsourced purchasing, it is impractical to list a price for every line item being supplied, so prices are given for a sample of items. So here's the scam: everything that was not a line item is charged at an exorbitant profit. Items not held in stock that have to be purchased from other suppliers are rarely line items in the bid, so while the contractor may pay £50, the customer gets charged way in excess of that, sometimes double (if you have any doubts just follow the invoice trail between suppliers, contractors and the customer).

If that isn't bad enough, the large suppliers (the 'big boys') know that their customers will process invoices without any knowledge of the work done, so borderline and not so borderline fraudulent bills are frequently passed through the system without question. As in the examples of providers of electronic tagging and work programmes, when exposed, such occurrences are always blamed on 'a few bad apples' and, in the case of central government suppliers, a period of 'corporate renewal' is all that is required to get back to business as usual. The truth is that the Whitehall 'thought collective' is wedded to the 'big boys'; they are the only ones that fit the political agenda of size, scale and 'professionalism'.

These scams operate in part because the contract prices agreed are based on unit costs. But it is not unit costs that matter. I shall return to housing shortly, but permit me a brief diversion into procurement policy generally.

Whitehall believes that fortunes can be saved by centralising procurement. "We all buy rubber gloves, bathrooms, catheters, whatever. So let's buy them centrally — that'll save on administration, and we can get a better deal." It has been a perennial cry throughout the time I have been involved with the public sector. Every year brings a fresh initiative in this vein. But the savings are a mirage. The bureaucracy associated with central buying can't handle the fact that while some things are cheaper, many are not, that some organisations want to support local suppliers, that despite the promise of efficiency, administrative costs rise rather than shrink, and so on.

But the real Achilles heel in procurement is the dogged assumption that what matters is unit cost. But this is just one more example of the false promise of economies of scale. The critical factor in managing supplies is not unit cost, it is time — the interval between purchase and use.

Think about it in practical terms. Buying stocks of rubber gloves or bathrooms at bulk rates may seem like a bargain, but it ignores the fact that they then have to be stored. There are costs associated with storage. It's not just the cost of space: items get soiled, they get lost, they get plundered for parts, all of which add to cost. Suddenly they don't seem so cheap any more.

The secret of cutting the cost of materials is to purchase them at the rate of use.

The pioneers of the Vanguard Method in housing repairs have learned how to do that, and the resulting fall in costs is breathtaking. On many items the unit cost is higher, but the overall cost of materials falls as the storerooms empty out. The first of the pioneers developed a software package that uses historical data to predict when materials will be needed, and they are bought on that basis, the users determining how many days supply they want to keep[1].

This is what happens when you manage flow, not cost. It is a profound innovation that is available to other suppliers to housing organisations. Yet because of the supposed professionalisation of procurement, small contractors, who have the nous and incentive to manage in this way, rarely get a look in.

The rise of professional procurement has associated with it a rise in legal claims on contracts awarded, because the big companies can afford to go to court. To avoid the threat of legal costs housing organisations have passed procurement to outsourced purchasers who know nothing about housing repairs. They work to what their customers tell them is 'best practice', which means targets, the schedule of rates and performance-related pay. (If you have jumped into the book here, you will have to read what's wrong with these things elsewhere; best to start with Chapters 8 and 9).

The big companies have no interest in managing the flow of materials — and it is easy to see why. Their organisations have a hierarchy of managers who get bonuses based on revenue and profits; the dodges I describe above are the means they use to gain enormous rewards.

It is ironic, to say the least. The drive to professionalise procurement began because of concerns (in housing repairs) that local builders might be giving backhanders. The wads of money in contractor managers' pockets are large and (mostly) legal, if on the edge of immorality. Procurement has created a system that legitimises parasitical gain and can only make backhanders more generous.

More generally, professionalising procurement leads to behaviour between the parties that, despite the rhetoric, institutionalises lack of trust, creates conflict and puts the interest of the recipients of services — customers — last, if that is they get considered at all. Meanwhile, lack of trust leads to more frequent procurement, and thus more work for the 'professionals'. Another disturbing feature is the growth of 'service' organisations that act as intermediaries in procurement. In essence they represent man's ingenuity at work — getting around the legislation by establishing 'framework' agreements (which avoid the need for further tendering) between providers and customers and, of course, taking a fee for doing so; which can only result in the customer (taxpayer) paying more. A zero-value disease.

We need urgently to abandon procurement legislation. To go back to where we started, what are the risks in managers having the freedom to choose their supplier and making a record of the reasons? They won't be greater than the risks in carrying on as we are.

The irony is that housing organisations dutifully following Whitehall's prescriptions will indeed have done a risk analysis, but they will still know nothing about the risks I have described here. These are risks that are designed in; not things that 'could go wrong' but things that 'are going wrong'. I turn to risk management next.

Chapter 23: Risk management

In his aptly titled book *Organised Uncertainty*[1], Michael Power describes how risk management has taken hold in modern organisations. To put it plainly: when as a manager you have carried out your approved risk identification, probability matrices, impact assessments, contingency planning and a host of other activities to define and manage the risks you face, documented your processes and actions and had them audited by outside experts, you still won't have a clue about what's going to happen and how you will react to it next week. You're fully organised — and completely uncertain.

Risk management in the public sector was cheer-led by Tony Blair[2]. Acknowledging the fact that the public sector had had its fair share of failures, he concluded that better management of risk would lead to fewer of them. As well as helping to avoid shocks and crises, risk management would foster innovation and change, he believed, promising guidance defining 'best practice', 'skills development' and a risk 'standard'.

Failures were taken as evidence that organisations are out of control, which may be the case, but does risk management improve control?

In 2001 the Treasury had produced *The Orange Book* — principles and concepts for the management of risk (rejecting the notion of a standard), revised in 2004[3]. *The Orange Book* defines risk as "uncertainty of outcome". Good risk management will "increase confidence in achieving outcomes, constrain threats and help people exploit opportunities, giving stakeholders increased confidence in the organisation's corporate governance and ability to deliver".

Herewith a flavour of *The Orange Book's* guidance:

"The level of risk remaining after internal control has been exercised (the 'residual risk') is the exposure in respect of that risk, and should be acceptable and justifiable — it should be within the risk appetite."

Clearly risk management will need the services of a facilitator who knows what this is supposed to mean, an 'expert' on whom managers can rely to counter the risk of getting their risk management wrong.

The Orange Book departs — as Blair did — from the commonly-held view that risk is only about things going wrong. It also sees risk in failing to take a positive opportunity, although it offers no illustration of what this means in practice. One example, however, is provided in the National Audit Office's earlier report on risk titled 'Supporting Innovation'[4]. For the NAO, there is a risk in or of failing to take opportunities to deliver more services digitally. Risk management is thus another stick with which to enforce compliance (in this case with an increased risk of failure).

As well as being mind-bendingly indecipherable, the guidance is tautological. The first thing to do is to identify risks. How? By identifying risk. But how, you may ask, do you work out what could go wrong? How can you know? No guidance there, but plenty of guidance on processes to follow, matrices to build, new language to use, and many unsubstantiated claims for the benefits that will accrue.

Predictably, risk management has created a self-perpetuating industry. Who would dare to say they don't care about risk? Leaders are encouraged to engage in processes which will give them the appearance of acting as if they know the risks they face. It reflects the political and managerial desire to maintain the myth of control and manageability (and also to demonstrate when something goes wrong that that it wasn't our fault — look, here's a list of boxes ticked to show we have taken all the approved precautions). The plausible idea is that if we make risk auditable and controllable, we can manage it. Once again, it is a delusion.

The risk industry scares leaders with solemn warnings of the terrible dangers of 'reputational risk'. While the celebrated case of Gerald Ratner is regularly trotted out (Ratner scuppered the jewellery chain of which he was chief executive by making the undoubted mistake of informing the world his shops sold 'crap'), neither banks nor telecommunications companies have suffered greatly from their appalling reputations, which have had little or no impact on customer retention. Dreadful reputations for customer service have not prevented private-sector suppliers from being invited to take on public-sector contracts or services, and even real reputational damage has had little practical effect — in the extreme cases of mistakes or malfeasance, companies merely had to feign a period of 'corporate renewal' to have their reputations (and contracts) restored.

Risk management was thought to provide immunisation against failure. A daily drip-feed of news of delay, cost overruns and cancellations to public-sector projects, many of them mentioned in this book, argues to the contrary. Likewise in the private sector, where risk management was unable to prevent the implosion of Enron, the Deepwater Horizon oil spill and the banking crisis, to name three of the most egregious cases. Meanwhile, not only has risk management had no discernible impact on the rate of failure, it has created a culture of defensiveness in which sensible judgement and common sense are the first casualties. Police officers who pleaded lack of training to justify failure to enter the water to rescue a child were defended by their superiors for observing the risk protocols; health and social care services are, too, plagued by defensive adherence to protocols. As I explained in the chapter on procurement, organisations taking the most defensible approach to outsourcing housing repairs are at the greatest risk of being ripped off, although at no risk of being castigated by the risk police. Defensible process will only increase the risk of complaints and thus complaint management, simply because of the problem I discussed earlier: protocols and standardised services won't absorb the variety of demand.

Risk management has become its opposite, a means of avoiding responsibility. It creates a massive carbuncle of organisational administration, a bureaucracy of control that is pure illusion, adding no value to the enterprise and, worse and even more Kafkaesque, blinding managers to the truth that current thinking about operational controls (targets, best practice and so on) is itself a huge source of risk, as I illustrated in Chapter 9 and elsewhere.

Risk management sets out to improve what, these days, is called 'governance' — in simpler language, control. But none of the ways in which current thinking about control is causing services to spin out of control is surfaced by the processes of risk management. Voices pointing to the negative effects of targets are ignored, whistleblowers are vilified even while risk management guidance blithely insists on the importance of being sensitive to signals. But signals that challenge current beliefs will be systematically ignored.

Analysis of disasters often shows that people knew what was happening well before the crises hit. A number of people saw and warned of the approaching financial crash. One, Paul Moore, head of financial risk management in a bank, was sacked for doing his job[5]. It is the same in the public sector — as countless examples show, speaking up, pointing out a problem or risk, is not welcomed. The failures in child protection are just one disturbing example[6].

Blair had argued that risk management in public services would transfer risk to the private sector while making public services more innovative. Every one of the recent failures will have been able to tick the boxes on risk management, while hiding the truth that the real risk was outsourcing public services on a payment-for-activity basis. Do you imagine this is being talked about in risk committees?

Uncertainty is the enemy of risk management; uncertainty renders risk management both futile and sterile. Knowledge is the antidote to uncertainty, at least for the things that we can get knowledge about, things that are in our control. We will never know all the risks we face, but we can do much to deal with what goes wrong, which will diminish all kinds of risk.

Asking a better question

The question we should ask is not, 'What could go wrong?' — the risk management question — but instead, 'What does go wrong?' And that can only be satisfactorily answered through getting knowledge.

In service operations this is to ask things like:

- · 'How often is a tradesman unable to carry out repairs on the first visit?'
- · 'How many people can't get their housing benefit resolved in two visits?'

- 'How often do people return to hospital when they shouldn't have?'
- 'How often do scene-of-crime officers attend events where their efforts provide no value?'
- 'What is the level of failure demand?'
- 'How many people who call NHS Direct have to go elsewhere to solve their problem?'
- 'How many services are duplicated when looked at from the users' point of view?'

When you frame questions about what does go wrong, think in terms of the purpose of the service from the customer's point of view, then you have to find the answers by studying.

When you know that is going wrong, it is important to ask a second question:

- 'Is this failure predictable?'

Predictable failure is under management's control. As a feature of the system, it can be tackled through changing the system. When leaders go after things that are going wrong predictably, the consequences are improved service and lower costs — and another effect is lower risk, at least in operations. A risk that is increased, however, is political; you have to be prepared to get out from behind the shield of defensive compliance, as failing to adhere to regulations is risky in itself.

When catastrophic failure occurs, we should ask:

- 'What happened?'
- 'Could it have been predicted?'
- 'Was it predicted?
- 'Why were the predictions ignored?'

The Queen asked why no one had predicted the economic crisis — but people did. I am confident that we will find that most crises were foreseen, but our antennae weren't tuned to that frequency. Stories about 'creaming and parking' were widespread before the Work Programme failures became common knowledge. Countless voices, including mine, have pointed out the flaws in the implementation of Universal Credit[7]. The problems in Staffordshire were and are common across the NHS; Staffordshire only gained publicity because local people would not be shut up. The catastrophically costly problems I described in outsourced housing repairs (Chapter 23) are, as I write, well-known; it is only a matter of time before a crisis is declared.

This is what risk management ought to be about: not asking questions about 'risk' but asking questions that lead to knowledge, reducing uncertainty rather than trying to manage it. Knowledge is the productive side of the risk-management coin.

There is one more big irony here. Risk management grew from the perceived need to staunch failures in public services. In its application not only has very little been learned about the causes of failure, but those described in this book have been hidden from view. Yes, risk management has made services more risky.

Chapter 24: Lean

The last few years have seen a never-ending stream of conferences and Whitehall publications promoting 'lean' in the public sector. Conferences are opened by ministers (who then depart, for what have they to learn?) and promoted by Whitehall departments. 'Lean' is extolled as a means to efficiency and better service. Nothing could be further from the truth.

Lean is represented as being the Toyota System in a box. The Toyota System was, in its day, a revolution. In the 1950s Toyota in Japan learned how to produce cars at the rate of customer demand, cutting out inventory. Even more remarkably, it managed to manufacture a variety of cars on the same production line while also improving quality. That stood in direct contrast to mass production methods employed until then and was astonishingly more efficient. Quality really is cheaper.

But who called the Toyota Production System 'lean'?

The term was coined by a member of the team behind the international research on car manufacturing, the results of which were published in *The Machine that Changed the World*[1]. It was thus promulgated as representing the Toyota System as a whole.

What did Taiichi Ohno, the man who developed the Toyota System, say about giving it a name? He was unequivocal: he warned against any kind of label on the grounds that managers would expect it to come as a ready-made package. He was right about that. The common approach to improvement is training people and getting them to do projects. That's why lean took off.

In short, lean reduced the Toyota Production System to a set of tools. In consequence, there is now an abundance of lean training in the tools, with accreditation for levels of competence and all the paraphernalia you would expect with a fad. But it is fading. Private sector service organisations are giving it up — the rudder of profit at work again. What they are learning, aside from the fact that the promised savings from the lean projects don't filter through to the bottom line, is that you can't change a system with a set of tools.

What was Ohno's view of tools?

Ohno counselled, 'never codify method', because it is thinking that is the key. His favourite word was 'understanding'. Tools are solutions to problems; does anyone imagine the problems Ohno had to solve in producing cars at the rate of customer demand are the same as those encountered in today's service organisations? Many seem to think the answer is yes, because the lean toolheads know no better, and the tools chime neatly with management's current (wrong) preoccupations. For example, tools are used to standardise work because managers assume that standardisation equates to efficiency. Yet as we have seen earlier, standardising work in a service organisation lessens the capability of the system to absorb variety, and thus can only drive costs up.

To sum up, the reason lean has become so popular is that it reinforces current thinking about management rather than challenging it.

How did Ohno teach his managers?

Unlike for today's lean salesmen, training managers in the application of tools and using them to solve their imagined problems was anathema to Ohno. On the contrary, he insisted that they start by figuring out what their real problems were, and that required study. Famously, Ohno would draw a chalk circle on the factory floor and tell his managers to stand there and study the system in action, on the ground. Managers would be left to study for weeks. Ohno never explained[2]. And here's the point: you can only absorb counterintuitive truths by studying and seeing them yourself. If you are *told* counterintuitive truths the kneejerk reaction is rejection ('of course standardised work is more efficient... it's obvious, the alternative is anarchy').

When we engage with new private-sector clients who have spent millions on lean projects, we often start by taking the leaders on a journey of discovery. We take a lean project that reported savings and have them study the service as a system. What they learn helps them see the folly of the lean intervention and, more importantly, the real scope for improvement.

The good news is that it doesn't take long for the scales to drop from their eyes. I have seen countless lean initiatives focused on making processes more efficient in departments where the demand is wholly failure demand. As Peter Drucker once said, "there is surely nothing quite so useless as doing with great efficiency what should not be done at all[3]. To take just one example, QUEST was a lean programme for the police. A joint exercise between the Home Office and a major consultancy, it aimed to speed up labyrinthine processes in the back office (see page 27). But, as readers will have come to expect by now, when you design a police service that works, most of those processes become redundant. Just by looking at demand and considering performance from an outside-in point of view, people working on projects like these discover they have a fundamentally different set of problems to solve, problems which require the full and diligent application of management intelligence, not a set of tools.

Lean will take longer to be abandoned in the public sector; but it is on the wane[4].

Chapter 25: IT – Features over benefits

In previous chapters on IT I have described the extent and reasons for IT failure and offered a better way to think about using it. In service operations the better way simultaneously reduces IT costs dramatically while getting more value from it. Everything we know about IT ought to make us extremely cautious. While it may be true that it is impossible to run a service operation without some sort of IT, it is certainly possible, and advisable, to run it with a great deal less.

My other previously-made point is that the IT industry is disinclined to dwell on (or even admit to) the ubiquitous failure of large IT projects, preferring instead to move rapidly on to promote the 'next big thing'. That IT companies succeed in selling these ideas represents a triumph of 'features' (what the latest innovation can do) over 'benefits' (what it does that makes things better). IT innovation is truly faddish: plausible but fuzzy ideas pushed by large marketing budgets on unwary lemmings who follow the herd.

Take, for example, the 'cloud'. There is no 'cloud' as such; it is merely a new way to share computing power and storage online. The 'new' feature is that users pay only for the resources they use — but 'cloud' sounds sexier. The unwary should be cautious about the sales patter and, ultimately, the deal; agreeing to contracts when out of your depth can be risky, especially when the salespeople are incentivised. But before chasing clouds we should be asking how much we really need large-scale processing power.

IT industry spokespeople are in no doubt: we need as much as we can get. It is the present and future. Local authorities are being showered with propaganda. Some examples:

"Citizens' interactions with local authorities are increasingly conducted online; every one of those contacts generates new data about the person using the service."

Does it? Actually, a large proportion of those contacts provide evidence that the services are not working. The 'new data' points to service issues rather than illuminating the characteristics of users.

"As more and more public services go 'digital-by-default', public bodies will have access to greater amounts of raw data about the citizens' lives, service choices and even personal habits."

The raw data will tell us more about the services we have provided than about the citizens' choices and views of the world, something digital services are poor at picking up. In any event, 'digital-by-default' is guaranteed to fail (see later).

Flogging their version of nirvana, the IT consultancies will tell you that:

"in the retail world, organisations would use this data to tailor services to individual users".

What this means is they will track what you bought, make assumptions about you, and then promote related goods to you. I bought a pair of walking boots on the internet, so now I get showered with offers of tents, camping stoves and so on. I hate camping. Now I dislike the internet service provider, too.

Before he left Tesco, then CEO Terry Leahy made an important discovery: what people bought may not have been what they wanted. The Tesco store card registered what customers bought in the shops, but when they began to order over the internet, he could see for the first time what they wanted that Tesco didn't stock.

Passing rapidly over the inconvenient lack of evidence for their claims, the IT companies project a future where 'data mining' can be used to 'improve service efficiency, prioritise and effectively enhance individual user choice, drive new demand and nudge citizens towards new behaviour'. I wouldn't bet on it.

What I would bet on, however, is that those gullible enough to follow the advice will incur significant costs associated with, in IT-speak 'compiling', 'structuring' and 'accessing raw data', let alone 'refining' and 'analysing' it, before they have any idea whether doing so can actually help them improve their business.

The IT companies want you to rent space on big machines ('the cloud') to deliver your strategy for 'Big Data', the label that has come to represent all of the above.

Big Data

Big data has its origins in surveillance data captured by the intelligence agencies about who talks to whom in cyberspace — surveillance as business model, as it has been described. Having established the feasibility of 'mining' large data sets, IT companies are promoting big data as the 'new oil'. In some examples cited it is an extension of the idea (above) that data mining can be used to build detailed profiles of customers and thus improve the way products are marketed (pushed) to them; web browsing habits, for example, could help marketing departments to improve the accuracy of their targeting. However, the gargantuan nature of the data sets means that only specialist analytic tools like parallel-processing software, algorithms for machine-learning and pattern recognition will do the trick, in effect making marketers dependent on the scarce specialists who have mastered these technologies.

Big data is enveloped in an aura of evangelism, hype, uncertainty and fear of being left behind. The promise is that it will unlock new knowledge, opening up ways of improving healthcare, tackling poverty, improving governance, revitalising democracy and combating global warming. Mmm[1].

One much-quoted example of big data in action was the prediction of a flu epidemic by tracking Google searches for the term. The claim was quickly de-bunked[2]. Another was the use of a smartphone app to detect and report potholes to Boston City Hall. We know from experience that it is possible to design an effective repairs serve that obviates all need for an app[3] — and indeed for any complex IT. Boston's app simply demonstrates the insensitivity of its service to demand — every signal from it registers failure demand.

Going back to the marketing hype, the IT industry eagerly claims that a 'click' on the internet is the same as a statement of intent or value.

But it is not, it is only a click. We can't tell why someone clicked or what value means to them in their terms. Making this mistake may have far worse consequences than showering walking-boot buyers with junk mail. Shortly after the Boston marathon bombing in 2013, someone searching online for pressure cookers and backpacks received a visit from the police.

The evangelists are now spreading the gospel to local authorities, using ideas dreamed up in marketing suites that can be sold as 'evidence'. So we see claims like:

> '*Accident and emergency patient data might indicate a rise in trips and fall injuries focused on a town centre street.*' The data should be '*traded with the local highways authority — perhaps in exchange for forward planning information about works that might increase A&E demand*'.

> '*Data mining could be used to understand networks of neighbourhood care and home-watch for the elderly*'.

> '*A critical benefit of the new technology is it allows organisations to get a much more sophisticated picture of true demand.*'

Except that it doesn't. IT systems are very poor at understanding demand, especially when it comes to people services. As an example, look at the debacle of Universal Credit (see Chapter 6), which is trying to roll a number of different benefits (and types of demand) into one. Recent announcements about UC have tellingly dropped references to 'digital by default' (of which it was to be the flagship) and now talk about 'multi-agency sites' (meaning bringing in people with the expertise to help, something that would have happened quickly and without red tape in my 'insurance' proposal (see page 45)), and experimenting with social media, wi-fi in libraries, one-to-one helpers and many other things[4].

UC appears to have moved from 'digital by default' to 'we don't know how to make UC work, but will try everything'. I'm sure by the time you are reading this the story will have moved on again.

The view that insight comes from analytics and data mining reinforces the notion of management as a remote activity, a matter of envisioning and strategy that can be handed down from on high. But good services, as we have seen in Chapter 10, are local, designed against demand, and employ *people* to absorb the variety.

Yet digital services remain a Whitehall obsession. Of course it is true that if you can deliver a service digitally, it will cost less to deliver than over the phone or face-to-face. The key word in that sentence is 'if'. Digital services work when demand is predictable, simple and repeatable, as with TV licences, car tax and the like — although even in these cases there are exceptions which cause digital channels to fail. Computers are not viable means of service delivery when demand has high variety, Universal Credit (Chapter 6) and care services (Chapter 10) being illustrations.

In June 2014 Francis Maude, minister for the Cabinet Office, insisted that elderly people will have to go online on pain of losing access to services. Maude thinks 'that is a better thing for people's lives'[5].

Non-computer-literate oldies ('refuseniks', as Maude calls them) will be able to apply for a one-off lesson to help them use the internet. Likening public service to buying airline tickets, he believes that services like carers' allowances will be capable of being provided online.

Naturally, voices of concern have been raised about elderly online competence, but that is the smaller problem. The larger problem is that any service with high variety of demand will fail, and there won't be the usual telephone or face-to-face service to mop up the failure demand.

Asked by the *Daily Telegraph* if all government services would eventually migrate online, Maude replied: 'Our point is that everything that can be delivered online, should be delivered online and only online.'

And this is the point: online services only work when the demand is predictable and straightforward. Regardless of the evidence, employing computers for things that people do better is a mistake that ministers never tire of making. What computers are good at, and should be used for, is storing information and making calculations. What they are extremely bad at, and on no account should be used for, is understanding and building relationships with people.

Social media

The analytics brigade is wooing local councils with promises that social media will be 'one of the best sources of new data' to generate 'social intelligence'. Oh, really?

Social media companies face a dilemma. Users find value in them. Will they find value in being targeted by advertising, having their data analysed and sold on to others, or finding their browser viewing determined by a computer's idea of what they want to see?

As yet we have no knowledge of successful applications of big data to services. What we *do* know is that IT advances always overpromise and under-deliver on real benefits, often at high cost. Believing the hype, many private-sector companies rushed to create their own social media pages as a means of 'engaging' their customers. Very few customers felt the need to 'engage' — no value there — but on the other hand irate ones discovered to their glee the power of social media to amplify their grievances and get them attended to in double-quick time. The message could hardly be more obvious: companies don't like being criticised in public. What were the knowable and unknowable costs in finding that out?

Social networks make their money from advertisers who seek large populations to aim their offers at. In the hype, companies were told they needed 'fans' (without explaining why) and then found it was almost impossible to address them without buying advertising.

Fans are people who have 'liked' your social media pages. It shouldn't come as a surprise that there have been reports of social media companies paying low-cost labour, working in 'click farms' and armed with fake social media accounts, to create lots of 'likes'[6].

Leaders of private-sector service organisations are now questioning the value of their social media initiatives. Projects have been unable to demonstrate any value. There are doubts that they will even achieve much, and they carry high risk of unintended consequences.

When is social media of value?

We can only answer that question by understanding value as defined by the user. So, for example, social media was used to powerful effect amongst protesters in the Middle East and rioters in the UK. It is easy to see the value to the users.

Adopters of social media will adjust their behaviour according to the value created for them, but there is no research in this area. From my observation, early adopters made what they now think of as excessive use of the new medium and now limit their use to solving specific problems, like issuing an invitation to a group of friends or passing messages and photographs. Clearly, social media can spread waves of attention, trending or Twitter-storms in Twitter-speak. But we have also seen how people resent tweets that are promotional, especially if they have been disguised as something else.

Before launching into ambitious spending on social media, big data and the cloud, it would be advisable to study what can be learned from experience so far, and what might be useful avenues for experimentation.

One experiment *we* could conduct would be to see how far social media can influence politicians about the issues raised by this book. Those of you who tweet might like to tweet politicians; maybe we could get it trending.

Part 5: Change must start in Whitehall

Introduction

Politicians don't know much about management: and nor should they.

Since the Thatcher era, politicians have placed themselves at the helm of public-sector reform. Regardless of party, their ideas have been much the same — ideas which, when we get down to the nitty gritty, are themselves the principal cause of rising cost and expenditure.

It is unrealistic to expect politicians to be experts in management. But that being so, they need — to put it bluntly — to recognise it and do the logical thing: get out of management altogether. This is *the* key change required in the way Whitehall tries to run public services if we are to realise the enormous opportunity that exists to improve those services.

In meetings with politicians I am often asked, 'If the ideas you describe work so well, why aren't all local authorities using them?' Consider the scale of the challenge. Leaders wanting to put them into practice must not only be prepared to change the way they think; to stand out from their peers by whom they will, potentially, be thought of as bonkers; but also to face down suspicion if not outright opposition from those — including regulators, civil servants and politicians — who command power and resources and are firmly wedded to a very different (that you now know as wrong) set of ideas. Given all that, we should be astounded at the number of leaders who *do* defy the odds to employ these methods. Over time their number will only grow as, once they cross the Rubicon, converts never go back to the old way of thinking.

Whitehall and its instruments of compliance — regulators and inspectors — ensure that what is done in the name of improvement is what fits the official narrative, what the minister agrees with. Tony Blair famously said that 'what matters is what works'. But actually what matters to Whitehall is conformance to the narrative. As I outlined in Chapter 1, there has been and remains a political consensus on public-sector reform. The current Whitehall narrative can be summarised as follows:

· Demand is and will go on rising, so budget reductions will mean a stark choice — either decommission services or reduce costs through cutting overhead or using more IT.

· Short-term salami-slicing is necessary but not sufficient.

· Public services have to move to lower-cost (digital) channels, and administrative (back-office) costs must be driven down through shared services and economies of scale.

· Expectations of public services must be managed downwards and citizens must take greater responsibility for their own wellbeing.

· Competition and choice will be important market levers.

· Further privatisation will drive down costs.

In sum, in the absence of further resources, the task is to manage public-service decline.

As I have illustrated, a better, positive, way exists, but it is hard to countenance for others since it directly counters this narrative.

In Part 5 I explain how Whitehall needs to change if it is to realise the necessary sea-change in thinking about and delivering public services. Firstly politicians need to be more circumspect about economic theories and economists; then, consistent with our approach to change, we need to understand why Whitehall is systemically incapable of 'doing evidence' such that, lastly, we can see how Whitehall can realise the opportunity at hand.

Chapter 26: Beware economists bearing plausible ideas

Spending time in Whitehall, you gain a clear impression that economists are the *eminences grises*. In yesteryear, politicians shared a broad consensus in favour of Keynesian economic thought with its emphasis on the importance of aggregate demand[1]. Since the 1980s it has shifted to neo-liberalism[2], at the heart of which is a belief in the efficiency of the market and, thus, consumer 'choice'. Wherever the consensus rests, the underpinning ideas are taken as axioms; economic theories somehow become economic truths. Economists advise governments and influence policy. Economics has its own Nobel Memorial prize. Commentators, even radio presenters, treat being an economist as a badge of pride. The rest of us are tacitly encouraged to believe that economics is the fount of knowledge, the saviour of the world. Economists are sages. As Keynes put it: "The ideas of economists and political philosophers, both when they are right and when they are wrong, are more powerful than is commonly understood. Indeed the world is ruled by little else."[3]

But here is the most incredible thing: while their powerful ideas rule the world, economists openly criticise the adequacy of their subject, frequently pointing out, as Keynes put it, when they are wrong. I can't think of another subject that expresses such vociferous self-doubt.

In *The Death of Economics*, Paul Ormerod described orthodox economics as an "empty box", the basis of which is "deeply flawed", and that "very little of the content of (economic) textbooks is known to be true"[4].

For Australian economist Steve Keen, "for over a century economists have shown that economic theory is replete with logical inconsistencies, specious assumptions, errant notions, and predictions contrary to the empirical data". And: "When their critiques are collated, little if anything of conventional economic theory remains standing."[5]

A glance in any library or bookshop will disclose an array of books with titles debunking economics. Yet we remain wedded to the ideas they doubt.

All governments since that of Margaret Thatcher have been wedded to the neo-liberal concept of free markets as key to economic prosperity. It's plausible; there's theory to back it up. But when I find myself surrounded by red-blooded capitalists I like to put this question to them: 'When did national economies grow the most, when subject to protectionist measures or operating as free markets?' The answer is not what they expect (protectionism, in case you doubted). Just one of Ha-Joon Chang's *23 Things They Don't Tell You About Capitalism*[6].

Hearing the answer, no one responds by saying, 'that's worrying'. Most people reply to the effect that the conditions must have been different, that free markets will ultimately prevail and so on. They have been conditioned to believe: capitalism good, protectionism bad. They are, as Keynes put it, slaves to an idea:

> *Practical men, who believe themselves to be quite exempt from any intellectual influences, are usually the slaves of some defunct economist. Madmen in authority, who hear voices in the air, are distilling their frenzy from some academic scribbler of a few years back... It is ideas, not vested interests, which are dangerous for good or evil.*[7]

Politicians would certainly see themselves as practical people, but are they (even if inadvertently) madmen in authority?

Economists lament that, as much as they want it to be, economics is not a science. Science is concerned with the development of knowledge; knowledge is the prerequisite for being able to predict — a capability that economics notoriously lacks. Mervyn King, former governor of the Bank of England, declared bluntly: "We can't predict the future, and we probably can't prevent more crises from happening"[8]. When Prakash Loungani, an economist at the IMF, reviewed the accuracy of economic forecasting in the 1990s, he concluded that "the record of failure to predict recessions is virtually unblemished". Extending the exercise to September 2008 (the date of the economic crash), he again found that no forecasters predicted it[9].

In response to the Queen's question about why no one foresaw the economic crash, Chicago economics laureate Robert Lucas explained that the crisis was not predicted because economic theory predicts that such events cannot be predicted[10]. Notwithstanding this kind of disdain for practicalities exhibited by many economists, there *were* people who predicted the crash (as I pointed out in Chapter 23).

Despite their failure to predict, that is to say work from a basis of knowledge, with few exceptions economists blame policy shortcomings on policymakers and policy implementers rather than on their own economic theories. As Keen puts it: "[economists argue that] the occasional failures of economies to react as economic theory predicts occur because the relevant policymakers applied the theory badly, or were using out-of-date economics"[11]. And John Kay puts it this way: "people blinded by faith or ideology have pursued false premises to absurd conclusions — and... come to believe that those who disagree are driven by 'woeful ignorance or intentional disregard'"[12]. One of the few economists to come clean about policy was Friedrich Hayek, darling of the right, who called his Nobel Memorial lecture in 1974 'The pretence of knowledge'. Conceding that "as a profession we have made a mess of things", he blamed the failure of economists to guide policy more successfully on 'scientism' — "their propensity to imitate as closely as possible the procedures of the brilliantly successful physical sciences — an attempt which in our field may lead to outright error"[13].

If economics is in such an openly dire state, how is it that economists have become so influential? In his book *The Worldly Philosophers*[14], Robert Heilbroner provides the key: their role has been to explain. Imagine you are a monarch or political leader in the days before we even used the word 'economics'. You want to raise more taxes. Someone points out that towns with machinery-based crafts generate more in taxes: that's one useful person to have around. As economic activity developed, other important questions arose. As towns begin to exchange goods, what to do about common weights and measures? As production expands, how do we deal with the impact on traditional producers, the guilds, which are now threatened? As the new industrialists become more economically powerful, how will the threat to those who hold power, the landowners, be managed?

As it happens, the answer to the last question was initially to take measures keep industrialists in their place, since the landowners — the aristocracy — were also the dominant parliamentarians. In consequence, industrialists started entering parliament.

In the evolution from a feudal system into something resembling a modern economy, many other issues needed to be addressed: the conflict between work as apprenticeship in guilds and tied labour (serfdom) and the new condition of workers being untied; the threat of imports; the impact of factories on human welfare; the distribution of wealth and power. Later, questions of boom and bust, internationalisation of capital, taxation, unionised labour and, of course, financial crashes would arise, alongside many others.

In their time, for the leaders of the day, these were all novel problems in uncharted terrain. Mistakes in dealing with them could have huge consequences. So someone able to explain, clarify, interpret or justify events, or provide intellectual order, would be an important asset. Economists claimed to do that. Not surprisingly, governments created institutions to develop, promote and protect what they thought of as a new branch of knowledge.

But a little economic knowledge can be a dangerous thing. Perhaps politicians should have heeded the words of another 20th century economist, Joan Robinson: "The purpose of studying economics is not to acquire a set of ready-made answers to economic questions, but to learn how to avoid being deceived by economists"[15]. Ironically, parroting its axioms ('competition requires choice and voice') constrains thinking and narrows choice; all because the axioms were, at some time, useful explanations. Explainers give solace and encouragement; such people also tend to be bright, interesting individuals.

Economists' tentacles reach deep into public-sector reform, providing plausible explanations which politicians turn into 'narratives'. The current narratives feature markets and competition, economies of scale, privatisation, separation of buyer and seller, leading to outsourcing, commissioning and procurement. If there is separation of the buyer and seller (the internal market), then market theory requires a regulator. The economists' notion of man as a rational (self-interested) actor led to the ideas of choice, targets, incentives, payment for results, performance-related pay and personal budgets. Acknowledging the weakness in the evidence for 'rational man', economists (in their now fashionable 'behavioural' variation) gave us 'nudge'.

There is also solace for politicians on the thorny issue of how to achieve reform, especially in the light of some spectacular failures. The economist most associated with public-sector reform, because of his closeness to Blair and subsequently the coalition, is LSE's Julian Le Grand[16]. In his book, *The Other Invisible Hand: Delivering Public Services through Choice and Competition*, Le Grand argues that public-sector reform has a choice between four strategies: trust, targets, voice and choice; his conclusion is that each has its place, its advantages and disadvantages. Evidence on the problems with any of the four strategies is treated as indicating the need for careful thought or dismissed as not critical and/or irrational. Politicians reading Le Grand are armed with arguments and counter-arguments, the stuff of their lives — all grist to the mill for those whose metier is talking.

One of Heilbroner's revelations is that the greatest economic thinkers — all people who were trying to understand the problems of their time — were not actually trained as economists. Today's students are astonished to find their tutors don't have answers to recent economic problems[17]. Today's economists, perhaps desperate to distance themselves from the aura of the 'dismal science'[18], extend their reach to all sources of ideas. Economic historian and philosopher Philip Mirowski describes how economists are "gleefully encroaching upon the spheres of interest of other disciplines"[19]. 'Nudge' encroached on social psychology but limited the borrowing to palatable studies that fitted with the politicians' desire to get 'them' to change 'their' behaviour. 'Nudge' ignored the important research on motivation (available from the same stable), perhaps because it is not a good fit with the narrative. Mirowski goes on to say, echoing Hayek, that economics is "a social science so promiscuous in its avidity to mimic the tools and techniques of other disciplines that it has no principled discrimination about what constitutes just and proper argumentation within its own sphere".

Borrowing from theories of motivation, Le Grand postulates that people are either 'knights' or 'knaves'[20] — knaves need carrots and sticks, knights can be trusted. He acknowledges the risks of sticks (not knowing that carrots can also have risks), but considers that treating all the players in reform as knaves might be the least-worst solution. No doubt treating everyone as knaves plays better politically than trusting people.

Wherever the political position, the holder will be armed with the arguments, but will not have gained real knowledge. They will argue for a cure or a disease without being able to discriminate between the two. Rather than treat the idea of knights and knaves as wisdom, politicians would do well to study and understand what we know about human motivation.

Channelling the energies of man into productive economic activity requires an understanding of how systems interact with and govern behaviour, something early economists understood:

"You can make of human beings what you want. The way he is governed commends Man to good, or to evil. The advantage of the nation must be the advantage of its members. He who separates advantages is an ignorant who damages the public body." So wrote J. F. von Pfeiffer in 1777[21].

Beware economists bearing plausible ideas.

Chapter 27: Whitehall is systemically incapable of doing evidence

Most politicians can't accommodate better management — even when they see it.

Providing evidence: housing services

In 2004 I was approached by a civil servant in the Office of the Deputy Prime Minister (ODPM, now the Department for Communities and Local Government). She said she'd heard about Vanguard's innovative work in housing and wanted it researched and reported on so that it could have some visibility in Whitehall. I said that nothing could be easier: just send civil servants to localities where we had been working so they could see what had been done. She told me it didn't work that way. Instead she would convene a panel that would oversee us working with housing organisations 'piloting' the method. As that was the requirement, I agreed.

The panel included the Audit Commission's chief inspector of housing, the director of regulation from the Housing Corporation and the ODPM's housing efficiency adviser. Three housing organisations, two from local government and one social landlord, agreed to be guinea pigs. Each piloted a different service: responsive repairs, voids (empty properties) and re-housing and rent collection / debt recovery.

During the pilots, panel members saw for themselves how targets acted to make performance worse in all services. We have already seen the effect of targets in housing repairs (Chapter 8). The panel discovered that targets for rent arrears, as another example, focused on the wrong end of the process. Through refocusing on the front end (how people were set up to pay), rent collection improved and arrears dropped in consequence.

In one of the pilots, the panel learned that using the local authority's centralised call centre (which ticks the regulator's box for sharing and lowering transaction costs) cost the housing organisation £250,000 a year for call-handling that added nothing of value to the service delivery. They also saw great results in all of the pilots.

When the pilot programme was over a report was compiled[1]. And what did any of the panel members do to follow up or build on the evidence acquired? Nothing.

The minister calls: housing repairs

By 2012 our work in housing had moved on. While in 2004 we were helping services to carry out repairs better and faster, boosting productivity, by 2012 we (more accurately the clients) had developed a design that provided tenants with a repair on the day and at the time they chose (if BT could do that we'd all cheer!). Grant Shapps, minister for housing at DCLG, had visited Portsmouth, the first to achieve this level of innovation, for which they were awarded a prize by Gary Hamel[2]. Shapps saw for himself how the design not only knocked tenants' socks off but also showed remarkable reductions in costs. He witnessed how this tenant-focused service begat an unintended consequence: tenants, who had now a positive view of the council, also engaged more responsibly in looking after their environment.

What was Shapps's response? A matter of weeks after his visit he announced his brand new initiative: tenants should be able to do their own repairs! Anyone with knowledge of housing legislation would know that this is plain daft. The landlord has a duty to ensure the property is safe, so any DIY work would now have to be subject to a bureaucracy of inspection and control.

Meeting the minister: adult social care

In 2006 I met Ivan Lewis, then Labour's minister for adult social care and David Behan, head of the Commission for Social Care Inspection (CSCI). I explained what we had learned by studying how adult social care worked in a council in the West Midlands. Failure demand was running at 86%, despite meeting regulated targets the true end-to-end times for conducting assessments were shockingly long, applicants re-presenting were being treated as 'new cases', administrative processes were labyrinthine and organised around meeting targets, and many of the services provided were standardised, so there was no thermostat in the system. Although the government's stated strategy was to "reduce need and enable", the consequences of the service in action were to extend needs and disable. The time spent on filling in forms to comply with regulatory requirements for the Department of Health, Audit Commission and CSCI, and others, was nothing short of astonishing.

They were shown how the service had been redesigned. The FACS (Fair Access to Services) criteria had been abandoned, every person who put their hand up for help was seen, and services or other assistance provided to help them maintain independence and dignity. Assessment times had been slashed and services were tailored to individual needs and delivered quickly. As a side-effect, social workers' morale had soared. As service improved as a consequence of the new design, costs were falling out of the system, demonstrating that it costs much less to help people when they are first in need. We wrote all this into a report[3].

What was the response of the minister and the regulator to this message of optimism and hope? They told me they were focused on the government's pledge to increase the take-up of personal budgets.

Some months after my meeting with the minister, the council in question learned that a CSCI inspection was imminent. Adult social care had a heavy weighting in the overall star ratings, and the council was 'defending' a four-star (top-rated) ranking. Rather than have the unconventional care arrangements endanger his stars, the chief executive ordered the adult care service to return to the inspection-safe, orthodox but wholly dysfunctional previous design.

Evidence and the Whitehall machine

Why does the regime react (or not react) the way it does? At first sight this is puzzling. Sometimes civil servants say that the government can't be seen to promote one consultancy, but that was not the purpose of sharing the evidence. And it isn't true, anyway; the big consultancies have been providing interventions through 'matched funding' in local authorities and police services, but, of course, these interventions fit rather than deny the narrative[4].

Viewing Whitehall from the inside, however, the reasons it can't deal with evidence become clearer. Beneath ministers there exists an enormous crowd of intelligent (and mostly young) people whose job is to develop policy. Their craft is informed by masses of inputs: evidence, opinion, think-tank research, academic papers, field visits, anecdotes; even television programmes[5].

The job of these bright young things is to sell policy ideas to the hierarchy which functions as a filter for the minister, judging the value of policy ideas by their fit with the minister's narrative and, importantly, how the idea might be defended when he/she is quizzed by the media. Impact and cost (both hard to assess) are also important, meaning that big numbers — often seemingly plucked from the air — win through. Many of the ideas that get through the filter, as we have seen, are those promoted by big consultancies, which often helpfully second staff to departments and fill top jobs in change and regulatory agencies.

Discussions with civil servants on public-sector reform are dominated by what they call 'agendas', these being the things their department has chosen to do in policy terms. DCLG officials talk endlessly about 'transformation' or 'localism' agendas without being concrete about what such things actually mean. Attendees at meetings often share opinions; but rarely do they share evidence. Regardless, the intelligent youngsters' purpose is to use the input to create narratives for their department's agendas, so anything that doesn't match the agenda, whether evidence or opinion, is politely ignored. Despite constant invocation of the word 'evidence', stressing its importance, their role ensures they only look for evidence they want to see.

Working closely with ministers to deliver their agendas gives officials an air of self-importance, as if expecting deference from their audience. They speak in generalities — 'people really care about the challenges facing local government' and 'people are interested in the localism agenda', 'we must leverage better outcomes', 'is there anything ongoing we can piggyback on?', 'cross-cutting budget themes'. Frequently it is hard to decipher what, exactly, they are talking about.

If an outsider turns the tables and points to the big issues within Whitehall, for example the ultimate need to get central government out of the silos that run all the way down to where service is delivered and create the fragmentation that is so costly, their reaction is to smile condescendingly and say, 'that won't be happening any time soon'. It is hard to imagine much of value coming out of such discussions. There is no sense that civil servants are cognisant of the dire state of services and passionate about improving them on the ground; their energy is focused on policy-making. Their priority is the policy agendas of ministers and departments, not citizens who need services.

Evidence fed into this system that doesn't fit the dominant narrative is either categorised as 'opinion' or simply rejected. Policy is 'what the minister agrees with'. For this reason the ideas that *do* fit with the narrative are promulgated widely (for example digital-by-default, shared services and outsourcing). And when it happens that the evidence shows the ideas aren't working, there is no change because evidence of failure doesn't challenge the overall narrative. Either the evidence must be wrong ('get some new evidence'), or implementation was faulty ('it'll work if we do it better').

Meeting the regulator: Audit Commission

It is not solely ministers who exhibit myopia. Stephen Bundred was the chief executive of the Audit Commission in the latter years of the last Labour government. At that time he attended a presentation I gave in London; the audience was understandably excited, whispering to me that he was present at the back of the room. It was during the period that the Audit Commission was bullying local authorities to share back offices in housing benefits, and housing benefits featured in my presentation. Following the presentation Bundred left; the only way to exit was to pass me, at the front of the room, which he did, assiduously avoiding eye contact.

We met again at the end of his tenure. It was at a round table organised by a public-sector magazine. I took the opportunity to speak to him directly as the event was finishing. I asked first of all whether he considered himself a public servant. He agreed he was. Then I asked, if he was told that there were flaws in what his organisation was doing and that there might be a better way of carrying them out, was it not his duty, as a public servant, to find out more? His reply was: "I just don't agree with you, John".

It doesn't matter who you are, arguing against the narrative will fall on deaf ears. Conservative backbencher Richard Bacon was joint author of a powerful dissection of the failure of IT-led reforms in government agencies[6]. The evidence he presented fitted with the theses here: IT-led change is doomed to fail; IT-dominated scale designs create services that don't work because they fail to absorb variety. It could have been a wake-up call, causing ministers and policymakers to revisit their strategies; but it changed nothing (except perhaps ensuring that the author remains on the back bench), and certainly not the narrative.

While parliamentary select committees have often done sterling work in exposing the folly of misguided reform initiatives, they have no teeth and seem to have no impact whatsoever on ministers who treat them as they would a grilling from journalists, defending their record rather than taking part in a dialogue which might throw new light on what they are trying to achieve.

A researcher for the Society of Local Authority Chief Executives (SOLACE) wrote a well-researched account of the fallacy of targets as means for control[7], but it cut no ice.

Countless organisations in the voluntary sector have protested about the disastrous effects of recent reforms on previously effective, often locally-based, services. Close to the ground, they knew what worked; they are astounded and dismayed at what has been put in their place. But no amount of noise gets Whitehall's attention.

Despite the claim to value evidence-based policy, Whitehall instead does policy-based evidence[8]. Compliance with policies is taken as evidence of their efficacy. Ideas are 'doomed to succeed', 'pilots' are rarely seen to fail (however badly they perform in practice) and morph seamlessly into fully fledged programmes. Not surprisingly people become cynical, seeing pilots as a way of softening them up for the change that's coming anyway.

Think about it. Is it logical or rational to expect politicians appointed to a position of power to assume expert wisdom overnight? One of the qualifications for a minister is that he or she should be able to master the new brief at speed. How is that possible? Isn't it foolishness to assume that a newly-appointed minister will be able to assemble in one brain the collected knowledge, wisdom and experience of all the souls working in a department? Why should a raw, newly-appointed minister have the answers to a department's long-running problems when their predecessor(s) with the same civil servants didn't? Ministers, only having a short time in office, are under pressure to do something quickly to get noticed; civil servants are promoted for success in getting policies through rather than implementing them (having a stake in whether they are right or wrong).

Think about it another way. If a minister determines a policy to which he or she is going to hold others to account, what is the risk that it will diminish discretion, judgement and responsibility, and/or simply be the wrong choice? As they themselves would say scornfully about public service, you wouldn't run a whelk stall like this. In a situation in which ministers arbitrarily determine answers to complex policy issues, it will be a matter of luck if the chosen course works, and even if by chance the directives are right, the culture of inspection and compliance will exclude all possibility of innovation in execution.

Ministers need to get out of management. We need to shift the locus of control.

Chapter 28: Getting a focus on purpose

Politicians should get out of management. But they should have a lot to say about purpose.

Let me remind you of the relationship between purpose, measures and methods.

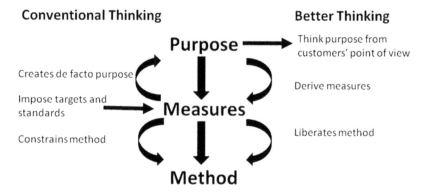

Purpose, measures, method: a systemic relationship

The relationship is systemic. For good or ill, it is at work in every organisation.

It is the imposition of measures and methods by politicians and regulators that is responsible for poor-quality public services, high costs and a culture of compliance that stifles innovation. 'Best practice' in the service of big ideas promulgated from the centre and inspected for compliance is in fact worst practice, a nail in the coffin of innovation.

For innovation to flourish, as we need it to, the locus of control must shift from the centre to the front line where people deliver public services. Innovation requires freedom to learn and experiment; it can't happen if it is constrained by consensus and regulation, especially when that consensus is largely developed among people with no knowledge.

The Whitehall ideas machine must go. It is at the heart of the current malaise and in truth is a disservice to ministers, entrapping them in a situation where they always need to be right, hate to have their opinions challenged, and are obliged to lay down the law — sometimes literally. Since politicians are systematically incapable of admitting they 'got it wrong', it makes sense to design a system where they are least likely to *be* wrong.

Politicians should limit their focus to the purpose of public services, something that is properly their responsibility to mandate. The rule, as I have argued, is that purpose must be thought of in customer (citizen) terms. Conceiving it this way puts politicians where they need to be: connected to the people they represent, able to appreciate the value of public services in their terms, to see sub-optimisation in terms of failure to work (meet the purposes) from the citizen's point of view, but also to understand how better services build stronger communities, resolve social problems and lower costs. Policy should be treated as an opportunity for experimentation in order to learn.

Leaders of public services should be required to work to the purpose of their services as defined by politicians and Parliament and then be freed up to determine the measures and methods to employ to meet those ends. This is not the anarchy it might look to some. On the contrary, working within the framework provided by a clear, robust statement of purpose, leaders will be responsible for the management choices for which they can be properly held to account. It is a far smarter, more productive form of control.

Freedom requires confidence that Whitehall will maintain constancy of purpose. Innovation in any endeavour occurs through trial and error. The more variation there is in terms of choices about measures and methods the greater the opportunity for identifying and understanding what works. Mistakes are part of the process, but they will be more easily spotted and far less problematic than those currently created (and often covered up), because they will consist of errors in practice rather than direction. As Russell Ackoff explained, when managers are doing the right thing less than perfectly, each correction makes them righter, whereas striving to do the wrong thing more efficiently just makes it worse[1].

Making leaders responsible for choices about measures and methods returns validity to inspection. Instead of inspecting for errors as laid down in checklists, inspectors will pose just one question: 'What are the measures and methods being used to achieve the purpose of the service?', and then check their validity. For the inspected organisation, this will entail no extra burden of preparatory work for the purposes of the inspector, as at present, since only the measures and methods in use will be in question.

This represents a shift from 'accountability' as compliance, as currently practised, to responsibility. It provides scope for discretion and judgement. It will be transparent to inspectors, politicians and citizens. It replaces a culture of compliance with a culture of innovation. Ironically, accountability will be improved as a result.

Intelligent regulation

Regulators must follow suit; their task is to regulate by and to purpose, avoiding any central specification of measures and methods.

It is time to re-think our philosophy of regulation. Regulations can only be justified if the controls they entail are economically and socially advantageous and, further, if the economic cost of regulating (administrative waste), doesn't outweigh the advantage (the reason for regulating in the first place).

The relationship between the value of regulation and its cost should have been the primary concern of European 'better regulation' task forces. Regulators need to face the fact that the current costs — knowable and unknowable — of regulation far exceed its value. In short, in many cases regulation provides no or negative value, often making services worse.

It is not the regulators' job to act as arbiters of good. Consider how the regulator responded to demonstrated improvements in food safety (see pages 94-95). The evidence showed that working to the regulatory requirements was a primary cause of sub-optimisation. The work was shown to a representative of the regulator, who while appreciating its value ruled that it needed validation from a higher source, which was forthcoming after a further presentation. At one level that could be considered a satisfactory outcome, but making it the prerogative of the regulator to authorise innovation is a brake on innovation and by no means guarantees that approval will be given.

Rather than treating the episode as matter for permission, the regulator could have interpreted it as a demonstration of the need urgently to address the value of the regulations. When findings of better service were shared with the regulator, again, nothing was done to build on the evidence. This is because regulators see their role as defining good and regulating for compliance. We experienced identical issues in work with children's services. Operating outside regulatory specification required authorisation, and the benefits of the better design cut no ice.

As we saw in the example of food safety, changing the methodology of regulation and inspection transforms the role of the inspector from policing to providing a welcome source of support. This is what intelligent regulation looks like.

A true focus on what works

With ministers focused on purpose, there is another key role for Whitehall: spreading and publicising 'what works'. 'What works' means proven, demonstrated and sustained change leading to significant, not marginal, improvement.

In publicising achievement Whitehall should limit communication to concise reports of results achieved, the problem leaders set out to solve and the problem that they actually solved (important as significant change is often a process of discovery that significantly changes the view of the problem faced).

Communication of method should be avoided as a precaution against recreating a culture of compliance. Success can only come from the study and understanding of method, which cannot be applied in a standard fashion like a set of tools. The first step in improvement is establishing the real problem, as opposed to the problem politicians imagined they had.

The road to improvement

The change I have described means a shift away from the central dictation of operating specifications such as targets, standards and activity. Instead, service leaders must be free to make responsible choices about the measures that will best enable them to achieve the purpose previously established by democratic political process. Freed from the obligation to deploy the paraphernalia of call centres, back offices, shared services, or outsourcing based on Whitehall's view of 'best practice', it will be up to public service leaders to choose how they improve their services against purpose, placing value on 'better practice', which is dynamic (anything can be improved) rather than 'best practice' which is static (as well as misleading). They will be guided by the rudder of efficacy, not the rudder of compliance — and they will be judged by the same token.

Such an approach recognises that the motivational engine for change is intrinsic (pride in doing the job well) not extrinsic (fear, carrots and sticks). Accountability will no longer mean compliance and reporting and spurious efficiency gains; instead, it will be transparently focused on improved effectiveness with lower costs as a result.

The opportunities are evident in every local authority and every public service in the land. What is standing in the way of taking those opportunities is a way of thinking. All that is required is for Whitehall to change the way it thinks.

Notes

The notes are here, not footnotes, so as not to interrupt your reading of the book. The vast majority simply provide sources for the statistics and references that I have quoted. If you want to follow any of the hyperlinks, the simplest way is to go to the online notes, from where you can click through to any of the urls shown here. The online notes are at: www.triarchypress.net/Whitehall/notes

Introduction

[1] From www.ukpublicspending.co.uk/recent_spending — 'UK public spending hit £150 billion in the mid 1980s and increased slowly to £180 billion in 1989. But then spending started to accelerate in the early 1990s, hitting £200 billion in 1990 and £284 billion by 1995. Increases in public spending were modest in the late 1990s, reaching £338 billion in 2000. The early 2000s showed an acceleration in spending, breaching £500 billion in 2006. Then the financial crisis of 2008 took over, boosting public spending over £600 billion in 2009. Public spending is expected to breach £700 billion in 2014.'

[2] Institute for Fiscal Studies, May 2010, *Election Briefing Note No. 5*, www.ifs.org.uk/bns/bn92.pdf

[3] Greg Clark, December 2012, *Decentralisation: an assessment of progress*, Dept. for Communities and Local Government (DCLG), p.4, www.gov.uk/government/publications/decentralisation-an-assessment-of-progress

1. Prelude

[1] See Anthony King and Ivor Crewe, 2013, *The Blunders of our Governments*, Oneworld, p.27 for details of the Blue Streak missile and Concorde projects.

[2] Margaret Thatcher, 1993, *The Downing Street Years*, Harper Collins, p.7: "The result of this style of accommodationist politics, as my colleague Keith Joseph complained, was that post-war politics became a 'socialist ratchet' — Labour moved Britain towards more statism; the Tories stood pat; and the next Labour government moved the country a little further left."

[3] Ibid. pp.12-13. She herself wrote "Our inspiration was... Hayek's powerful Road to Serfdom, dedicated to the socialists of all parties".

[4] Margaret Thatcher, 4 July 1977, 'Speech to Greater London Young Conservatives (Iain Macleod Memorial Lecture — "Dimensions of Conservatism")' From the Thatcher online archive: www.margaretthatcher.org/document/103411

[5] "'None of you can be any good' [Thatcher] once told the British Rail board over lunch, 'or you would be in private industry'." Simon Jenkins, 2007, *Thatcher and Sons*, Penguin, p.4.

[6] From the Thatcher online archive: www.margaretthatcher.org/document/103411

[7] Catherine Haddon, 2012, 'Reforming the Civil Service: The Efficiency Unit in the early 1980s and the 1987 Next Steps Report', Institute for Government, p.18. www.instituteforgovernment.org.uk/publications/reforming-civil-service-efficiency-unit

[8] Margaret Thatcher, 1993, *The Downing Street Years*, Harper Collins, p.608: "I said that the Department of Health and Social Security (DHSS) must make a real effort to respond quickly to the attacks on our record and the performance of the NHS. After all, we had increased real spending on the NHS by 40 percent in less than a decade."

[9] Ibid. p.607.

[10] Simon Jenkins, 2007, *Thatcher and Sons*, Penguin, pp.113-116 "[Thatcher] told the nation on the BBC's Panorama programme, apparently without consulting her health ministers, that the NHS should be totally reformed... The resulting blood-stained White Paper appeared in January 1989, claiming to be 'simulating within the NHS as many as possible of the advantages which the private sector and market choice offered, but without privatisation'."

[11] John Major, 2000, *The Autobiography*, Harper Collins, p.245.

[12] Duncan Campbell-Smith, 2008, *Follow the Money: The Audit Commission, Public Money and the Management of Public Services 1983-2008*, Allen Lane, pp.10-11 "Armed with ever more measures of performance, the auditors engaged with their audited bodies in new ways: league tables heralded a readiness to evaluate the performance of councils, relative to their peers across the country, against a set of centrally directed criteria."

[13] Under Blair, CCT was replaced with a new duty of 'Best Value' which was designed to "create the conditions under which there is likely to be greater interest from the private and voluntary sectors in working with local government to deliver quality services at a competitive price" — Dept. for Environment, Transport and the Regions (DETR) 1998, *Modern Local Government: In Touch with the People*, White Paper Cmnd 4014, clause 7.30.

[14] Duncan Campbell-Smith, 2008, *Follow the Money: The Audit Commission, Public Money and the Management of Public Services 1983-2008*, Allen Lane, p.11: "In

its third decade, the commission was expected to do more than illuminate the facts as in the 1980s, or point to underlying patterns as in the 1990s. It had to join with government in devising ways to effect real change. (It was an evolution labelled 'sight-insight-foresight' by those fond of such rubrics.) As this suggests, New Labour's continuing quest for a quantum improvement in Britain's public services posed a huge challenge for the Commission and its auditors — inviting them into a relationship with government that posed delicate questions for the independence of the Commission from government, always a far subtler matter than the statute-protected independence of the auditors from the audited."

[15] See Department for Transport, Local Government and the Regions (DTLR), September 2001, *Modern councils, modern services - access for all.* www.webhostingpal.com/lectures/apel/modern.doc

[16] Ibid, para. 3.7.

[17] Peter Gershon, 2004, *Releasing resources to the front line: Independent Review of Public Sector Efficiency,* HMSO.

[18] Audit Commission, 2007, *Environmental Scan: Efficiency of Back Office Functions in Local Government,* p.14: "ex-Cabinet Office Minister Jim Murphy is quoted as saying 'Departments that share corporate services such as HR and finance could create 20% efficiency savings'". http://archive.audit-commission. gov.uk/auditcommission/sitecollectiondocuments/AuditCommissionReports/ NationalStudies/backtofrontenvironmentalscan.pdf

[19] The Prime Minister's Strategy Unit. 6 June 2006, *The UK government's approach to public service reform.* http://webarchive.nationalarchives.gov. uk/20070701080507/cabinetoffice.gov.uk/strategy/downloads/work_areas/ public_service_reform/sj_pamphlet.pdf

[20] Cabinet Office, 2008, *Excellence and fairness: Achieving world class public services.* http://webarchive.nationalarchives.gov.uk/20081230001747/http:// cabinetoffice.gov.uk/media/cabinetoffice/strategy/assets/publications/world_ class_public_services.pdf

[21] Gordon Brown writing in the *Financial Times* 9th March 2008: "So this is my approach to achieving excellence: no tolerance of underperformance, giving users of public services more choices and, crucially, a new recognition that real and lasting change must come from empowering the users of services themselves, with professionals and government playing a supporting role. And all of this only possible, even in a more challenging global economic environment, by a long-term commitment to investment as well as reform in our public services." www.ft.com/cms/s/0/c96a2baa-edfc-11dc-a5c1-0000779fd2ac.html

[22] The work led by Martin Read was written up as HM Treasury, 2009, *Operational Efficiency Programme: back office operations and IT*. See http://webarchive. nationalarchives.gov.uk/+/http:/www.hm-treasury.gov.uk/d/oep_back_office_ pu730.pdf

[23] The 'scroungers' term appeared regularly in press comment pieces on the Mick Philpott court case. Philpott was jailed for his part in a house fire that left six of his children dead. "Welfare is there to help people who work hard, it shouldn't be there as a sort of lifestyle choice." — David Cameron, April 2013.
See: www.dailymail.co.uk/news/article-2304804/Mick-Philpott-benefits-culture-David-Cameron-backs-George-Osborne-saying-arson-case-raises-questions-welfare-lifestyle-choice.html

Cameron and his ministers contrasted a case like this one with government policies to support what they termed the 'strivers': "Where's the fairness for the shift-worker, leaving home in the dark hours of the early morning, who looks up at the closed blinds of their next door neighbour sleeping off a life on benefits... We speak for all those who want to work hard and get on... They strive for a better life. We strive to help them." — George Osborne, October 2012. See: www.newstatesman.com/blogs/politics/2012/10/george-osbornes-speech-conservative-conference-full-text

This became labelled the 'strivers versus skivers' debate in the media, with opposition politicians also using the term 'striver'. See: *The Guardian*, 'Skivers v strivers: the argument that pollutes people's minds', Wednesday 9 January 2013. Byline: Zoe Williams. www.theguardian.com/politics/2013/jan/09/skivers-v-strivers-argument-pollutes.

Part 1: The industrialisation of public services

2: Call centres

[1]"Failure demand: 'demand caused by a failure to do something or do something right for the customer'." John Seddon, 2003, *Freedom from Command and Control*, Vanguard Education, p.26.

[2] From *Hansard*, 'Written Answers to Questions' 21 February 2005, Col 337W Local Government. www.publications.parliament.uk/pa/cm200405/cmhansrd/ vo050221/text/50221w88.htm

[3] See a short animation about the DECATS process which aimed to simplify and standardise processes across local government at: www.vanguard-method.com/ content/691/

[4] *Hansard*, 24 February 1998, Vol 307, Col 155, The Secretary of State for Health (Mr. Frank Dobson) "We are to introduce NHS direct, and we are running pilot schemes from 1 April. We intend to have a scheme covering the entire country. People will be able to ring in to talk about their condition and receive advice from a nurse-organised help line. We believe that that will be effective and popular." www.publications.parliament.uk/pa/cm199798/cmhansrd/vo980224/debtext/80224-01.htm#80224-01_spnew10

Hansard, 9 July 1998, Vol 315, Col 1252, Frank Dobson: "'It is clear that many people are willing to ring the 24-hour helpline knowing that it is there for 24 hours. Some of them, because they are considerate of others, are reluctant to go to accident and emergency or ring for a doctor or ambulance. In some cases, people who clearly would not have rung for an ambulance have rung NHS direct and ambulances have been sent round straight away because the cases were urgent. In many cases, nurses have given immediate reassurance to concerned parents, the children of elderly parents and people worried about their neighbours. It has been a great success and I commend the people who have been carrying it out." www.publications.parliament.uk/pa/cm199798/cmhansrd/vo980709/debtext/80709-10.htm

[5] *The Times*, November 26, 2001, 'We need more time'. Byline: Alice Miles.

[6] See 'The Vanguard Method in Wellbeing' for more on failure demand in healthcare: http://wellbeing.vanguard-method.com/health-and-care-system-dynamics-video-series/

[7] James Munro, John Nicholl, Alicia O'Cathain and Emma Knowles, 2000, 'Impact of NHS Direct on demand for immediate care', *British Medical Journal*, 321:150-153.

[8] *The Telegraph*, 9 February 2011, 'The chequered history of NHS Direct'. Byline: Stephen Adams. www.telegraph.co.uk/health/healthnews/8313761/The-chequered-history-of-NHS-Direct.html

[9] *Health Which?* ,August 2000, 'NHS Direct Investigated' pp.12-16.

[10] BBC News, 12 June 2007, 'NHS Direct "a strain on system"'. Byline: Nick Triggle. http://news.bbc.co.uk/1/hi/health/6742473.stm

[11] *The Telegraph*, 24 October 2008, 'Every call to NHS Direct costs £25'. Byline: Kate Devlin. www.telegraph.co.uk/health/3253245/Every-call-to-NHS-Direct-costs-25.html

[12] Ibid.

[13] BBC Radio 4, 18 August 2013, 'Face the Facts'. www.bbc.co.uk/programmes/b0384815

[14] Ibid.

[15] *The Guardian*, 2 July 2013, 'NHS Direct pulls out of two 111 medical helpline contracts'. www.theguardian.com/society/2013/jul/02/nhs-direct-pulls-out-111-helpline

[16] Channel 4 Dispatches, 29 July 2013, 'Undercover in NHS 111'. Byline: Luke Denne. www.channel4.com/programmes/dispatches/articles/all/undercover-in-nhs-111

The Independent, 29 July 2013, 'NHS Direct aims to pull out of 111 contracts leaving non-emergency phone line on brink of collapse'. Byline: Charlie Cooper. www.independent.co.uk/news/uk/home-news/nhs-direct-aims-to-pull-out-of-111-contracts-leaving-nonemergency-phone-line-on-brink-of-collapse-8736270.html

[17] Her Majesty's Inspectorate of Constabulary (HMIC), 2005, *First Contact: A Thematic Inspection of Police Contact Management*, p.11:
"The growth of commercial and public sector call centres has been echoed in policing. In the last ten years, 33 of the 43 police forces in England and Wales have centralised or consolidated their call handling function, either physically or using technology to deliver a 'virtual' centralised contact centre service. Undoubtedly, the Best Value principles and the drive for economies of scale have played a large part in this move."
www.hmic.gov.uk/media/first-contact-full-report-20051101.pdf

[18] Audit Commission, 2002, *Learning from Inspection: Housing Repairs and Maintenance*. http://archive.audit-commission.gov.uk/auditcommission/sitecollectiondocuments/AuditCommissionReports/NationalStudies/housingrepairs.pdf

3. Back Offices

[1] John Seddon, 2003, *Freedom from Command and Control: A Better Way to Make The Work Work*, Vanguard Education.

[2] Richard B. Chase, 1978, 'Where does the customer fit in a service operation?' *Harvard Business Review*, Vol. 56 No. 4, pp. 137-42.

[3] W. Edwards Deming,1982, *Out of the Crisis*, MIT Press, p.134.

4. Shared Services

[1] John Seddon, 2010, 'Why do we believe in economy of scale?' https://www.vanguard-method.com/v1_lib.php?current=575

[2] National Audit Office (NAO), March 2012, *Efficiency and reform in government corporate functions through shared service centres*, Report by the Comptroller and Auditor General HC 1790 Session 2010—2012.

[3] Browne Jacobson, 2008, *Shared services survey 08: The Report*, with Foreword by Sir Peter Gershon, CBE www.brownejacobson.com/pdf/Shared%20services%20report_new_supplied_by_jj.PDF

www.conservatives.com, 2010, 'Cut Labour's waste to stop their tax rise on working people' http://www.conservatives.com/~/media/files/downloadable%20files/nic.ashx?dl=true

[4] HM Treasury, 2009, *Operational Efficiency Programme: back office operations and IT*, written by Martin Read. http://webarchive.nationalarchives.gov.uk/+/http:/www.hm-treasury.gov.uk/d/oep_back_office_pu730.pdf

[5] House of Commons Public Accounts Committee, 2008, *Shared Services in the Department for Transport and its agencies: Fifty—seventh Report of Session 2007—08*. www.publications.parliament.uk/pa/cm200708/cmselect/cmpubacc/684/684.pdf

[6] National Audit Office, 2011, *Shared Services in the Research Councils*, Report by the Comptroller and Auditor General HC 1459 Session 2010-12, 21 October 2011: "By March 2011, implementation costs totalled £130.5 million, exceeding the original budget of £78.9 million by 65 per cent, with some residual functionality still to be developed. On a best case, the project has reported gross savings to March 2011 of £27 million but is at least £73.2 million behind the business case projections and is expected to fall further in the future."

[7] ResearchBlogs, August 14 2010, 'Delpy says Shared Services Centre remains on track': http://exquisitelife.researchresearch.com/exquisite_life/2010/08/delpey-says-shared-services-centre-remains-on-track.html

[8] *Times Higher Education*, 23 August 2012, 'Shared Services Centre is "below standard" and new tasks won't help it improve, says STFC head'. Byline: Elizabeth Gibney. www.timeshighereducation.co.uk/420942.article

[9] Ibid.

10 For example, see blogposts at: http://fundermental.blogspot.co.uk/2010/09/rcuk-moon-rocks-kidnapped.html and at: http://fundermental.blogspot.co.uk/2011/11/jekyll-and-hyde-character-of-research.html

11 From Account NI, 2013, *Review of a Public Sector Financial Shared Service Centre.* www.niauditoffice.gov.uk/account_ni.pdf

12 BBC News, 14 May 2014, 'PAC says Account NI payment cost "extraordinarily high"'. www.bbc.co.uk/news/uk-northern-ireland-27398896

13 From Account NI, 2013, *Review of a Public Sector Financial Shared Service Centre* www.niauditoffice.gov.uk/account_ni.pdf

14 BBC Democracy Live, 23 January 2014, 'Auditor general criticises financial centre checks'. www.bbc.co.uk/democracylive/northern-ireland-25851212

15 *Public Finance*, 14 May 2014, 'Northern Ireland PAC slams costs of shared financial services scheme'. Byline: Vivienne Russell. www.publicfinance.co.uk/news/2014/05/northern-ireland-pac-slams-costs-of-shared-financial-services-scheme

16 Computing.co.uk, 7 June 2011, 'Savings from Somerset shared services falling well short of target'. Byline: Gareth Morgan. www.computing.co.uk/ctg/news/2076695/savings-somerset-shared-services-falling-short-target

17 *Public Finance*, 1 May 2011, 'All in this together?' Byline: Karen Day. www.publicfinance.co.uk/features/2011/05/all-in-this-together/

18 Ian Liddell-Grainger MP blog, 19 January 2012, www.liddellgrainger.org.uk/local/SOUTHWESTONE.html

19 *Western Daily Press*, 16 February 2012, '"Failing" Southwest One comes under fire from Somerset County Council leader'. www.westerndailypress.co.uk/Failing-Southwest-comes-Somerset-County-Council/story-15242751-detail/story.html

20 BBC Points West on Southwest One Review Report, 6 June 2011. www.youtube.com/watch?v=vKzSHxz14YI

21 *Local Government Lawyer*, 25 February 2014, 'Report into Southwest One pinpoints "incredibly complicated" contract'. www.localgovernmentlawyer.co.uk/index.php?option=com_content&view=article&id=17460%3Areport-into-southwest-one-pinpoints-incredibly-complicated-contract&catid=53%3Aprocurement-and-contracts-articles&Itemid=21

Contract exit costs were settled out of court for £5.9m, the council believed it might have had to pay as much as £40m if it had lost the case: www.bbc.co.uk/news/uk-england-somerset-23339493

22 HM Government, December 2012, *Next Generation Shared Services: The Strategic Plan*. www.gov.uk/government/uploads/system/uploads/attachment_data/file/83717/19284_Next_Generation_3rd_Online.pdf

23 NAO Press Release, 31 March 2014, 'Update on the Next Generation Shared Services Strategy' www.nao.org.uk/press-releases/update-next-generation-shared-services-strategy/

24 Amyas Morse, head of the National Audit Office, 7 March 2012: "The initiative for government departments to share back-office functions has suffered from an approach which made participation voluntary and tailored services to meet the differing needs of individual departments. The result was over complexity, reduced flexibility and a failure to cut costs. The new Cabinet Office strategy on shared services acknowledges these issues but, if it is to achieve value for money, it must learn the lessons from past implementation. Only in this way can the sharing of back-office functions have a realistic prospect of contributing towards the government's drive to cut public spending in the long term." www.nao.org.uk/report/efficiency-and-reform-in-government-corporate-functions-through-shared-service-centres/

25 The LGA published a map on 30 May 2014 which showed 337 councils across the country engaged in 383 shared service arrangements. The resultant claimed savings were £357 million. See: http://www.local.gov.uk/productivity/-/journal_content/56/10180/3511353/ARTICLE

26 *IT News for Australian Business*, 12 August 2013, 'WA to pay $370m to scrap Shared Services'. Byline: Allie Coyne, Paris Cowan. www.itnews.com.au/News/353082,wa-to-pay-hefty-cost-for-scrapping-shared-services.aspx

5. Outsourcing

1 *Birmingham Mail*, 12 June 2012, 'Call centre not to blame for frustration with Birmingham City Council services, claims report'. Byline: Neil Elkes. www.birminghammail.co.uk/news/local-news/call-centre-not-to-blame-for-frustration-186673#ixzz1xZjnDlCG

2 Service Birmingham call centre was taken back in house: See thechamberlainfiles.com, 24 June 2014, 'Service Birmingham costs to fall by £150m after Capita takes a 'pragmatic view' to council contract renegotiation'. Byline: Paul Dale. www.thechamberlainfiles.com/service-birmingham-costs-to-fall-by-150m-after-capita-takes-a-pragmatic-view-to-council-contract-renegotiation/

The cost of exiting the Service Birmingham contract remains "shrouded in secrecy": See *Birmingham Post*, 31 July 2014, 'Time for city to bite the bullet and save millions on its Capita contract'. Byline: David Bailey. www.birminghampost. co.uk/news/news-opinion/david-bailey-time-birmingham-bite-7543701

[3] *Computer Weekly,* 13 September 2005, 'Bedfordshire pays HBS £7.7m to terminate outsourcing contract'. www.computerweekly.com/news/2240075126/ Bedfordshire-pays-HBS-77m-to-terminate-outsourcing-contract

[4] BBC News, 17 July 2013 'Southwest One contract dispute cost council £5.9m'. www.bbc.co.uk/news/uk-england-somerset-23339493

[5] *Financial Times*, 3 November 2013, 'Whitehall outsourcing is "in our interests"'. Byline: Sarah Neville and Gill Plimmer. www.ft.com/cms/s/0/77039df2-4395-11e3-8279-00144feabdc0.html

[6] HM Treasury, 2009, *Operational Efficiency Programme: back office operations and IT.* Author: Martin Read (p.30, Chart 2.K: Cost efficiency journey, Source: Bain, McKinsey and PWC research provided to the Operational Efficiency Programme).

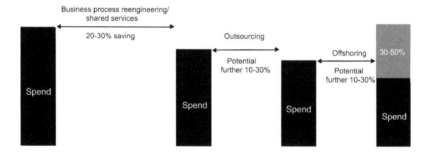

http://webarchive.nationalarchives.gov.uk/+/http:/www.hm-treasury.gov.uk/d/ oep_back_office_pu730.pdf

6. Information Technology

[1] Robin Gauld and Shaun Goldfinch, 2006, *Dangerous Enthusiams: E-government, Computer Failure and Information System Development,* Otago University Press.

[2] Outcomes from IT investments: 80-90% do not meet their performance goals; 80% are late and over budget; 40% of developments fail or are abandoned; fewer than 25% integrate business and technology objectives; just 10-20% meet all their success criteria. See:, OASIG, Institute of Work Psychology, 1995, *Failing to deliver: the IT performance gap,* University of Sheffield.

[3] House of Commons Committee of Public Accounts, 5 July 2013, *The dismantled National Programme for IT in the NHS, Nineteenth Report of Session 2013—14*, p.21. www.publications.parliament.uk/pa/cm201314/cmselect/cmpubacc/294/294.pdf

[4] "Tim Donohoe, Senior Responsible Officer for Local Service Provider Programmes (LSPs), insisted that the NHS had 'got a good deal for the taxpayer'... Donohoe said that the NHS couldn't pull out of the contract all together on the basis of a breach — despite not fulfilling its terms — because it could have claimed things about how the NHS conducted itself and it was agreed that it was 'not worth the risk of getting into further legal disputes'."

Quoted in *Computerworld UK*, 12 June 2013, 'NHS still set to spend £600m with "rotten" CSC on "hopeless" NPfIT systems'. Byline: Derek du Preez. www.computerworlduk.com/news/public-sector/3452333/nhs-still-set-spend-600m-with-rotten-csc-on-hopeless-npfit-systems/

[5] House of Commons Committee of Public Accounts, 24 June 2013, *FiReControl: Update report, Sixteenth Report of Session 2013-14*, www.publications.parliament.uk/pa/cm201314/cmselect/cmpubacc/110/110.pdf

[6] House of Commons Communities and Local Government Committee, 5 June 2006, *Fire and Rescue Service: Fourth Report of Session 2005—06 Volume I*. www.publications.parliament.uk/pa/cm200506/cmselect/cmcomloc/872/872i.pdf

House of Commons Communities and Local Government Committee, 16 March 2010, *FiReControl: Fifth Report of Session 2009—10*. www.publications.parliament.uk/pa/cm200910/cmselect/cmcomloc/352/352.pdf

[7] *Computerworld UK*, 23 July 13, 'MPs attack rescue plan for £482 million FireControl project'. Byline: Matthew Finnegan. www.computerworlduk.com/news/public-sector/3460263/mps-attack-rescue-plan-for-482-million-firecontrol-project/

[8] Dexter Whitfield, 2007 'Cost overruns, delays and terminations: 105 outsourced public sector ICT projects' ESSU Research Report No. 3 www.european-services-strategy.org.uk/news/2007/ict-contract-chaos/

[9] See www.gov.uk/government/uploads/system/uploads/attachment_data/file/246700/0283.pdf p43 and www.rpa.gov.uk/rpa/index.nsf/vDocView/F51B6B0D961521A7802570450051BAB9?OpenDocument 'Our net running costs in 2012—13, at £169m, were £5.1m higher than in 2011—12.'

[10] House of Commons Committee of Public Accounts, 14 November 2011, *Rural Payments Agency - follow up to National Audit Office and Public accounts Committee Recommendations - corrected evidence Corrected transcript of Oral Evidence HC 1616-i' Q167.* www.publications.parliament.uk/pa/cm201012/cmselect/cmpubacc/c1616/c161601.htm

[11] See a short animation about the Prince 2 project management methodology. Prince 2 leads to plenty of activity but little understanding and, hence, plenty of failure: www.vanguard-method.com/content/349/

[12] *New Statesman*, 19 February 2014, 'Is Cameron now afraid to mention Universal Credit?' Byline: George Eaton. http://www.newstatesman.com/politics/2014/02/cameron-now-afraid-mention-universal-credit

[13] Campaign4Change, 12 March 2014, 'Another DWP leader quits — is Universal Credit IT really working?' Byline: Tony Collins. http://ukcampaign4change.com/2014/03/12/another-dwp-leader-to-leave-is-universal-credit-it-really-working/

[14] *The Guardian*, 23 May 2014, 'Watchdog now treating universal credit as 'new project' after successive delays'. Byline: Patrick Wintour. http://www.theguardian.com/politics/2014/may/23/universal-credit-reset-iain-duncan-smith

[15] John Seddon, 'Dissolving a Dangerous Enthusiasm: Taking a Systems Approach to IT Systems', *Cutter IT journal* Vol. 26, No. 4, April 2013 https://www.vanguard-method.com/resource.php?res=918

[16] *The Independent*, 10 March 2014, 'Councils spend millions on controversial 'pseudo-science' lie-detector tests to help catch benefit frauds'. Byline: Ian Johnston. http://www.independent.co.uk/news/uk/politics/councils-spend-millions-on-controversial-pseudoscience-liedetector-tests-to-help-catch-benefit-frauds-9182629.html

[17] Ibid.

[18] "The group's first priorities, with immediate effect, will be to: ... implement an immediate freeze on all new ICT spend above £1 million; review the government's biggest projects, including ICT projects, to see where costs can be reduced or wasteful projects stopped altogether; start renegotiating contracts with major suppliers across government to reduce costs", from a gov.uk press release, 24 May 2010, 'Cabinet Office and Treasury to join forces to drive out waste': https://www.gov.uk/government/news/cabinet-office-and-treasury-to-join-forces-to-drive-out-waste

Part 2: Delivering services that work

Introduction

[1] This video shows leaders from organisations that have employed the Vanguard Method talking about their experiences: www.vanguard-method.com/v1_lib.php?current=906

7. A better philosophy

[1] BBC Radio 4, 4 January 2007 'In Business' Clip at 26.24 onwards: www.bbc.co.uk/radio4/news/inbusiness/inbusiness_20070104.shtm

8. Effective change starts with 'study'

[1] John Seddon, 2008, *Systems Thinking in the Public Sector: the failure of the reform regime and a manifesto for a better way*, Triarchy Press.

[2] The subscriber area of the Vanguard Method website provides practical applications of the VM, including video of experts and detailed descriptions of how to conduct 'check' and redesign services: www.vanguard-method.com

[3] Some people (I call them 'tool-heads') will tell you there are 7 types of waste. See for example www.institute.nhs.uk/quality_and_service_improvement_tools/quality_and_service_improvement_tools/lean_-_7_wastes.html or www.kaizen-training.com/tools-techniques/defining-value-and-the-7-wastes These were derived from the types of waste found in manufacturing organisations. To send someone out to find these types of waste — as is common in tool-head interventions — is a folly. Waste is anything that is not the value work; thinking about it this way you learn about your own types of waste.

9. Better thinking, better design

[1] See Denise Lyon and Andy Brogan, 'East Devon District Council Housing Benefits Transformed' and Anne McKenzie, 'Stroud District Council Systems Thinking Results In Housing Benefits' in Middleton, P (ed.), 2010, *Delivering Public Services that Work (Volume 1): Systems Thinking in the Public Sector Case Studies*, Triarchy Press.

[2] See Jo Lane and Phil Badley, 'Stockport Metropolitan Borough Council Implementing Systems Thinking in IT and HR' in Middleton, P (ed.), 2010, *Delivering Public Services that Work (Volume 1): Systems Thinking in the Public Sector Case Studies*, Triarchy Press.

[3] The journal *Systemic Practice and Action Research* devoted a special issue to the Vanguard Method including articles about applications in higher education, children's services and in a domiciliary care provider for adults with learning disabilities. See http://link.springer.com/journal/11213/27/1/page/1.

See also:

Charlotte Pell, 2012, *Delivering Public Services that Work (Volume 2), The Vanguard Method in the Public Sector: Case Studies*, Triarchy Press

John Seddon and Brendan O'Donovan, 2012, 'Process Innovation at Portsmouth Housing' in Macaulay, L.A et al (Eds) *Case Studies in Service Innovation*, Springer Science + Business Media

Keivan Zokaei, John Seddon and Brendan O'Donovan, 2010, *Systems Thinking: From Heresy to Practice*, Palgrave Macmillan.

A longer list of published examples can be found at: www.vanguard-method.com/v1_lib.php?current=794

10. 'Locality' working

[1] 'Locality and Vanguard 2014: Saving money by doing the right thing — Why "local by default" must replace "diseconomies of scale"' p.14. www.vanguard-method.com/v1_lib.php?current=907

More detailed notes on the nature of demand into housing allocations and the subsequent intervention can be found in the subscriber area of the Vanguard website: www.vanguard-method.com/media/855

[2] Rowena Crawford and David Phillips, 'Local government spending: where is the axe falling?' in Institute *for Fiscal Studies Green Budget February 2012*, p.126: Spending on social care amounts to £21.0 billion, 20% of local government expenditure. www.ifs.org.uk/budgets/gb2012/12chap6.pdf

[3] *The Guardian*, 23 March 2014, 'Stop bulk buying public services and save £16bn'. Byline: Neil Berry and Louise Winterburn. www.theguardian.com/public-leaders-network/2014/mar/13/bulk-buying-public-services-16bn-contracts

[4] 'Locality and Vanguard 2014: Saving money by doing the right thing — Why "local by default" must replace "diseconomies of scale"' p.14. www.vanguard-method.com/v1_lib.php?current=907

[5] Policy.Mic, 10 February 2014, 'The Most Unlikely State in America Is On Track to Eradicate Homelessness By 2015'. Byline: Emmett Rensin. http://mic.com/articles/81507/the-most-unlikely-state-in-america-is-on-track-to-eradicate-homelessness-by-2015

11. IT as pull, not push

[1] See www.vanguard-method.com/v1_lib.php?current=846 , a video where IT developers from a private sector organisation describe what they learnt from applying the Vanguard Method in their work.

[2] John Seddon 'Re-thinking IT', recorded 11 November 2010 at Øredev developer conference, Malmö, Sweden http://vimeo.com/19122939

Case studies have been published in:

John Seddon and Brendan O'Donovan, 2012, 'Process Innovation at Portsmouth Housing' in Macaulay, L.A et al (Eds) *Case Studies in Service Innovation*, Springer Science + Business Media

Peter Middleton and Brendan O'Donovan, 'Improving Software Project Management in Bureaucracies' in Keivan Zokaei, John Seddon and Brendan O'Donovan, 2010, *Systems Thinking: From Heresy to Practice*, Palgrave Macmillan.

[3] Sean Kennedy, 'The New Development Control service in Rugby: "Absolutely Bloody Fantastic"' in Charlotte Pell, 2012, *Delivering Public Services that Work (Volume 2), The Vanguard Method in the Public Sector: Case Studies*, Triarchy Press

[4] Sue White, David Wastell, Karen Broadhurst and Chris Hall, 'When policy o'erleaps itself: The "tragic tale" of the Integrated Children's System', *Critical Social Policy*, August 2010, vol. 30 no. 3 pp.405-429.

[5] Joanne Gibson and Brendan O'Donovan, 'The Vanguard Method as Applied to the Design and Management of English and Welsh Children's Services Departments', *Systemic Practice and Action Research*, February 2014, Volume 27, Issue 1, pp.39-55.

[6] ITIL is an abbreviation for the Information Technology Infrastructure Library. In the 1980s the UK Government's Central Computer and Telecommunications Agency noticed that government agencies and private sector contracts had started independently following their own IT management practices. It was believed that the development of consistent practices for all aspects of an IT service lifecycle could drive improvement in organisational effectiveness and efficiency and therefore lead to the achievement of predictable service levels. ITIL was thus developed as a set of recommendations for standard practices in IT. Today ITIL is widely used throughout the world as a standard for IT service management with guidance on how to plan, deliver and support IT service features such as service strategy, service design, service transition, service operation and continual service improvement.

[7] John Seddon, 'Dissolving a Dangerous Enthusiasm: Taking a Systems Approach to IT Systems', *Cutter IT journal* Vol. 26, No. 4, April 2013, www.vanguard-method.com/resource.php?res=918

Part 3: Things that make your head hurt

12. Targets and standards make performance worse

[1] John Seddon, 2008, *Systems Thinking in the Public Sector: the failure of the reform regime and a manifesto for a better way*, Triarchy Press.

[2] BBC News, 4 April 2014, 'Met Police has "culture of fear", officers say': www.bbc.co.uk/news/uk-26878761

[3] BBC News, 4 April 2014, 'Police performance targets "questionable"' First broadcast on Radio 4 Today programme, 4 April 2014: www.bbc.co.uk/news/uk-26881037

[4] *Evening Standard*, 4 April 2014, 'Police accused on "target setting"': www.standard.co.uk/panewsfeeds/police-accused-on-target-setting-9236688.html

[5] House of Commons Public Administration Select Committee, 9 April 2014, 'Caught Redhanded: Why we can't rely on Police Recorded Crime' Thirteenth Report of Session 2013—14 HC 670: www.parliament.uk/business/committees/committees-a-z/commons-select/public-administration-select-committee/news/crime-stats-substantive/

[6] BBC News, 10 September 2013, 'Theresa May warning over police targets "comeback"': www.bbc.co.uk/news/uk-24037125

[7] *Daily Mail*, 15 January 2014, 'How we can't trust the crime figures: After Plebgate, now watchdog says police statistics are unreliable'. Byline: James Slack. www.dailymail.co.uk/news/article-2540003/Its-official-Crime-numbers-NOT-trusted-statistics-watchdog-strips-police-data-seal-approval.html

[8] *The Guardian*, 15 January 2014, 'Police crime figures lose official status over claims of fiddling'. Byline: Alan Travis. www.theguardian.com/uk-news/2014/jan/15/police-crime-figures-status-claims-fiddling

[9] In the UK, a P45 is the reference code of an official tax form given out by employers when an employee leaves their employment. The term is used in slang as a metonym for termination of employment. For more on Selbie's role in making NHS waiting time goals known as "P45 targets" see *Financial Times*, 13 March 2010, 'How New Labour succeeded with NHS policy': www.ft.com/cms/s/2/168e1278-2b24-11df-93d8-00144feabdc0.html

[10] *The Telegraph*, 27 March 2014, 'Fears that hospitals are covering up death rates'. Byline: Laura Donnelly. www.telegraph.co.uk/health/healthnews/10728189/Fears-that-hospitals-are-covering-up-death-rates.html

[11] *The Sunday Times*, 16 February 2014, 'Patients sent home early cost trusts £390m'. Byline: Jon Ungoed-Thomas.

[12] *Health Service Journal*, 17 February 2012, 'DH: hospitals must be fined for readmissions caused by others'. By Crispin Dowler. www.hsj.co.uk/news/finance/dh-hospitals-must-be-fined-for-readmissions-caused-by-others/5041632.article#.U_dUqGMmvEk

[13] *The Sunday Times*, 16 February 2014 'Patients sent home early cost trusts £390m'. Byline: Jon Ungoed-Thomas.

[14] *The Telegraph*, 11 June 2014, '"Significant action" needed to meet missed A&E targets'. Byline: Keith Perry. www.telegraph.co.uk/health/10893676/Significant-action-needed-to-meet-missed-AandE-targets.html

[15] *Pulse*, 3 October 2011, 'Darzi centre providers paid compensation for early closure': www.pulsetoday.co.uk/darzi-centre-providers-paid-compensation-for-early-closure/12817392.article#.UahpsEDVDXU

[16] Steve Allder, 'Improved stroke care at half the cost' in Charlotte Pell, 2012, *Delivering Public Services that Work (Volume 2), The Vanguard Method in the Public Sector: Case Studies*, Triarchy Press

[17] Robert Francis, 2013, *The Mid Staffordshire NHS Foundation Trust Public Inquiry Report*. www.midstaffspublicinquiry.com/report

13. Inspection can't improve performance

[1] See www.vanguard-method.com/v1_lib.php?current=706 for details on analysing performance capability, and more on how to construct capability charts.

[2] See www.vanguard-method.com/content/345/ for more on mystery shopping, why it is dumb and the problematic behaviour it generates in service organisations.

[3] For a discussion about how CSCI (the Commission for Social Care Inspection) was imposing an enormous burden of inspection on council adult social care departments see John Seddon, 2008, *Systems Thinking in the Public Sector: the failure of the reform regime and a manifesto for a better way*, Triarchy Press, pp.141-142.

[4] Ibid. pp.82-84.

[5] Prior to the Baby P case, Haringey had been inspected by Ofsted and been awarded 3 stars. See *The Guardian*, 29 April 2010, 'The Baby P blame game reveals that social work reform has taken a turn for the worse'. Byline: Professor Sue White. www.theguardian.com/society/joepublic/2010/apr/29/baby-p-social-work-reform-backtracks

[6] The Healthcare Commission rated the Trust as 'good' in its 2006 report. See *The Independent*, 6 February 2013, 'Timeline: The Mid Staffordshire NHS Trust scandal'. www.independent.co.uk/life-style/health-and-families/health-news/timeline-the-mid-staffordshire-nhs-trust-scandal-8482726.html

[7] *The Observer*, 6 April 2014, 'Michael Gove's bid to limit fallout from failing free schools — revealed'. Byline: Daniel Boffey and Warwick Mansell. www.theguardian.com/education/2014/apr/06/michael-gove-failing-free-schools

[8] John Seddon, 2008, *Systems Thinking in the Public Sector: the failure of the reform regime and a manifesto for a better way*, Triarchy Press.

[9] Kate Watts, 'Food Safety in Great Yarmouth: An Adult Conversation' in Charlotte Pell, 2012, *Delivering Public Services that Work (Volume 2), The Vanguard Method in the Public Sector: Case Studies*, Triarchy Press.

14. Regulation is a disease

[1] Speech by Martin Wheatley, Managing Director, Financial Services Authority, (later to be known as the Financial Conduct Authority) 5 September 2012, 'The incentivisation of sales staff — are consumers getting a fair deal?' www.fsa.gov.uk/library/communication/speeches/2012/0905-mw.shtml

[2] Bob Rhodes and Richard Davis, 2014, 'Regulation: The unintentional destruction of intentional communities'. www.centreforwelfarereform.org/library/by-date/regulation.html

Simon Caulkin, 26 February 2014, 'Social care: who needs enemies?' www.simoncaulkin.com/article/428/

The Guardian, 30 July 2014, 'Communities for learning disabled residents face split after reform row' www.theguardian.com/society/2014/jul/30/camphill-learning-disabled-communities-split-row-reform-pay-values

[3] Robert Francis, 2013, *The Mid Staffordshire NHS Foundation Trust Public Inquiry Report*. www.midstaffspublicinquiry.com/report

[4] Single-loop and double-loop learning were patterns first described by Chris Argyris and Donald Schön. Single-loop learning involves improving incrementally

through learning new skills or capabilities, with managers perhaps learning to do something better but without challenging the underlying beliefs and assumptions behind their problems. Double-loop learning goes further than single-loop learning by reshaping the patterns of thinking and behaviour which govern why actions are taken. Double-loop learning is essential in the progression towards becoming a 'learning organization'. See Chris Argyris, 'Teaching smart people how to learn', Harvard Business Review, May 1991. http://hbr.org/1991/05/teaching-smart-people-how-to-learn/ar/1

[5] *The Telegraph*, 12 February 2013, 'Jeremy Hunt: "Let's cut nurses' paperwork by a third"'. Byline: Stephen Adams. www.telegraph.co.uk/health/healthnews/9863416/Jeremy-Hunt-Lets-cut-nurses-paperwork-by-a-third.html

[6] *The Guardian*, 6 February 2013, 'David Cameron's prescription for NHS failings: target pay of nurses'. Byline: Denis Campbell. www.theguardian.com/society/2013/feb/06/david-cameron-nhs-nurses?CMP=EMCSOCEML657

Sky News, 7 January 2012, 'PM Wants Nurses To Check Patients Every Hour'. http://news.sky.com/story/915579/pm-wants-nurses-to-check-patients-every-hour

[7] Jeremy Hunt MP, Speech to Reform Thinktank, 12 February 2013, 'An NHS that treats people as individuals'. www.gov.uk/government/speeches/an-nhs-that-treats-people-as-individuals

15. It's the system, not the people

[1] Joseph M. Juran (1904- 2008) taught 'Juran's Rule': "Whenever there is a problem, 85% of the time it will be in the system, 15% of the time it will be the worker" as quoted in Myron Tribus, 1993, *The Germ Theory of Management*, SPC Press. See www.vanguard-method.com/v1_lib.php?current=579

Similarly, Dr W Edwards Deming (1900-1993) taught that "The fact is that the system that people work in and the interaction with people may account for 90 or 95 percent of performance". See Deming quoted in Peter R. Scholtes, 1998, *The leader's handbook: making things happen, getting things done*, McGraw-Hill, p.296.

[2] John Seddon, 2003, *Freedom from Command and Control*, Vanguard Press, p.126.

[3] BBC News, 19 June 2012, 'Francis Maude: Shake-up "not attack on civil service"'. www.bbc.co.uk/news/uk-politics-18494800

[4] See www.vanguard-method.com/content/404/ for a video and articles on the subject of 'Culture change is free'.

[5] See www.youtube.com/watch?v=bcdahNIu820 for a video of a sales leader in a financial services company studying her team and seeing the '95/5' principle for herself.

[6] *The Sunday Times*, 9 February 2014, 'Trust charges taxpayer for private ops'. Byline: Richard Kerbaj.

[7] House of Commons Health Committee, 18 December 2012, *Health Committee 2012 accountability hearing with the Care Quality Commission*. www.publications.parliament.uk/pa/cm201213/cmselect/cmhealth/592/592we10.htm

16. Incentives always get you less

[1] Stuart Sutherland, 2007, *Irrationality*, Pinter and Martin.

Alfie Kohn, 1993, *Punished by Rewards: the trouble with gold stars, incentive plans, A's, Praise and other bribes*, Houghton Mifflin.

Edward L. Deci, Richard Koestner and Richard Ryan, 1999, 'A meta-analytic review of experiments examining the effects of extrinsic rewards on intrinsic motivation', *Psychological Bulletin* 1999 Nov; 125 (6):627-68; discussion 692-700.

[2] See www.vanguard-method.com/content/855/ for more on the subject of 'payment by results' and why it will always give you worse results.

[3] The famous 'Whitehall II' study found that a major cause of stress at work was an imbalance between the psychological demands of work on the one hand and the degree of control over work on the other. People in jobs characterised by low control had higher rates of sickness absence, of mental illness, of heart disease and pain in the lower back. See Council of Civil Service Unions/Cabinet Office, 2004, *Work stress and health: the Whitehall II study*. www.ucl.ac.uk/whitehallII/pdf/Whitehallbooklet_1_.pdf

[4] Daniel Pink, 2009, *Drive: The Surprising Truth About What Motivates Us*, Riverhead Books.

[5] Frederick Herzberg, 1987, 'One More Time: how do you motivate employees?' *Harvard Business Review.* Sept-Oct 1987 reprint with commentary of 1968 original (vol 46: no 1: pp.53-62).

Part 4: ideology, fashions and fads

17. Choice

[1] David Cameron MP speech 11 July 2011, 'Open Public Services': www.gov.uk/government/speeches/speech-on-open-public-services

[2] The paper cited by Cameron in his speech is: Zack Cooper et al., 'Does Hospital Competition Save Lives? Evidence from the English NHS Patient Choice Reforms' Working Paper No. 16/2010, first published in January 2010 by LSE Health: http://eprints.lse.ac.uk/28584/1/WP16.pdf

The paper was strongly criticised by Allyson Pollock and her colleagues in The Lancet, where the authors said that: 'Although Cooper and colleagues claim to examine the impact of patient choice, they do not ascertain whether choice significantly affected the destination of patients... Crucially, the study lacks plausibility because Cooper and colleagues produce no explanation of any causal mechanism or path by which choice of provider for elective care could have affected outcomes for AMI in the NHS... Far from showing that competition saves lives, at best Cooper and colleagues' study shows that people who have an AMI and whose GPs are close to a hospital or who have many hospitals in their area might have better chances of survival. The policy solution is therefore very different from that currently being followed.' See Allyson Pollock et al., 2011, 'No evidence that patient choice in the NHS saves lives', The Lancet, Vol. 378 December 17/24/31, 2011 pp.2057-2060.

[3] John Seddon, 2008, *Systems Thinking in the Public Sector: the failure of the reform regime and a manifesto for a better way*, Triarchy Press, p.24.

[4] These figures come from John Curtice and Oliver Heath, 2009, 'Do people want choice and diversity of provision in public services?' in Alison Park et al. (eds) *British Social Attitudes: the 25th Report*, Sage, p.60:

"For example, we asked our respondents to state which of a set of four possible priorities for the NHS was 'most important for the NHS to achieve'. No less than 78% chose 'make sure people who are ill get treatment quickly'. In contrast, just six per cent say 'make sure people have a lot of choice about their treatment and care', slightly less than the seven per cent who opt for 'make sure that people on low incomes are as healthy as people on high incomes', though rather more than the two per cent who choose 'get the number of people aged under 50 with heart disease down as low as possible'."

[5] John Seddon, 2008, *Systems Thinking in the Public Sector: the failure of the reform regime and a manifesto for a better way*, Triarchy Press, p.17.

[6] For example: Tom Gash and Theo Roos, 31 August 2012, *Choice and competition in public services: Learning from history*, Institute for Government: www.instituteforgovernment.org.uk/publications/choice-and-competition-public-services

The authors say: "One problem in assessing the impact of market mechanisms was the general lack of any systematic evaluation of whether competition in itself raises standards. Academics on our panels could point to indicative evidence from evaluations of different contracting models but were rarely able to highlight pilots which directly tested the benefits of contractual approaches versus in-house provision. This is partly due to the fact that reform (and refusal to reform) has often been driven by political concerns and ideology but it is also, no doubt, due to the technical difficulty, time and cost of such exercises."

Also the *New Statesman*'s rolling politics blog, 4 April, 2012, 'The problem with public service "choice"'. Byline: Prateek Buch. www.newstatesman.com/blogs/politics/2012/04/problem-public-service-choice

Buch says: "For every unpublished, non-peer-reviewed study that claims to show how choice and competition raise standards, you can find many rebuttals that expose methodological and empirical flaws. Take the now infamous studies claiming that competition for elective surgery (indexed not by a measure of choice itself but by geographic density of hospitals, a poor proxy at best) improves outcomes in mortality from heart attacks (through an unspecified mechanism); the papers show weak statistical correlations at best, not a causal relationship, and yet they're unquestioningly cited as evidence that 'hospitals in more competitive areas perform better on quality and efficiency than those in less competitive ones'."

[7] An NHS guidance paper from April 2014 says this: "New legal right to choice of mental health provider: From 1 April 2014, patients have a new legal right to choose the provider of their mental health services at first outpatient appointment, as they do in their physical health care." www.england.nhs uk/2014/04/03/bulletin-for-ccgs-issue-56-03-april-2014/#MHprovider

[8] Laird Ryan, May 2014, *NCIA Inquiry into the Future of Voluntary Services: Working Paper 5 Outsourcing and the Voluntary Sector.* http://t.ymlp336.net/mmbqafaubbsyagaejbarajwh/click.php

Other papers on the subject of the future of voluntary services are to be found on the National Coalition for Independent Action webpages at: www.independentaction.net

Additional evidence of the impact of commissioning on third sector organisations can be found in the report by Locality and Vanguard, *Saving money by doing the right thing: Why 'local by default' must replace 'diseconomies of scale 2014,* ', p.14. www.vanguard-method.com/v1_lib.php?current=907

[9] David Boyle, 24 January 2013, *The Barriers to Choice Review: How are people using choice in public services?*, Cabinet Office. www.gov.uk/government/publications/barriers-to-choice-public-services-review

18. Personal Budgets

[1] Liz Newbronner et al., 2011, *SCIE Report 40: Keeping personal budgets personal: learning from the experiences of older people, people with mental health problems and their carers*, Social Care Institute for Excellence: www.scie.org.uk/publications/reports/report40/

[2] Brendan O'Donovan, 2010, 'Systems Thinking in Adult Social Care: how focusing on a customer's purpose leads to better services for the vulnerable in society and enhances efficiency' in Keivan Zokaei, John Seddon and Brendan O'Donovan, (eds), 2010, *Systems Thinking: From Heresy to Practice*, Palgrave Macmillan.

[3] The New Economics Foundation (nef) has been at the forefront of the development of ideas of co-production in the UK with this working definition of co-production: "Co-production means delivering public services in an equal and reciprocal relationship between professionals, people using services, their families and their neighbours. Where activities are co-produced in this way, both services and neighbourhoods become far more effective agents of change." See http://coprod-network.ning.com/forum/topics/what-is-the-definition-of, http://www.neweconomics.org/publications/entry/co-production and the Wikipedia page on the subject here: http://en.wikipedia.org/wiki/Coproduction_%28public_services%29

However, it is hard to know how to translate this definition into something operational, i.e. by what method does one go about creating good co-production in practice?

19. Commissioning

[1] Rick Wilson, 'Living the Life You Choose: The Introduction of the Vanguard Method into an Organisation Providing Support to People with Learning Disabilities', *Systemic Practice and Action Research*, February 2014, Volume 27, Issue 1, pp.57-74.

[2] As presented by Karen Burton at the 'Better for Less' conference, 20 March 2014 at the ICC Birmingham. See Simon Caulkin's write-up of the event here: www.vanguard-method.com/images/Better%20for%20Less%2020th%20March%20Conference%20Summary.pdf

[3] Ann Anderson and Fred Parkyn, '"Design to understand" in health and social care' in Charlotte Pell, 2012, *Delivering Public Services that Work (Volume 2), The Vanguard Method in the Public Sector: Case Studies*, Triarchy Press.

See also a feature on BBC Radio 4's 'You and Yours' programme on the Somerset work here: www.vanguard-method.com/v1_libphp?key=you+and+yours&id=525

20. Managing demand

[1] Anna Randle and Henry Kippin, 2014, *Managing Demand: Building Future Public Services*, The RSA. www.rsa2020publicservices.org.uk/publications/managing-demand-building-future-public-services/

[2] *Western Morning News* (Plymouth) 26 February 2008 '"Computer says no" to contacting your council'. Byline: Matt Chorley.

See also *The Observer* 22 March 2009, '7 days: Pendennis: So much for open government' Byline: Oliver Marre. "Francis Maude, Tory Chairman, tells me he's discovered an official government policy of reducing 'avoidable contact' with the electorate (intended to speed up services and cut out timewasting, but it's not going to win much support from people who hope to be in touch with officials or make a complaint). Says Maude: 'The prime minister is cutting himself off from an angry and disillusioned electorate. He is following his own barmy Whitehall targets to the letter and avoiding contact with the public.'"

[3] Keivan Zokaei et al., 2010, *Lean and Systems Thinking in the Public Sector in Wales*, Lean Enterprise Research Centre report for the Wales Audit Office, Cardiff University, p.55. www.vanguard-method.com/resource.php?res=453

21. Nudge

[1] Richard Thaler and Cass Sunstein, 2008, *Nudge: Improving decisions about health, wealth and happiness,* Penguin.

[2] See the film 'Food Inc' 2008 (Dir: Robert Kenner) www.takepart.com/foodinc/film

[3] *The Washington Post*, 3 October 2011, 'U.S. touts fruit and vegetables while subsidizing animals that become meat'. www.washingtonpost.com/national/health-science/us-touts-fruit-and-vegetables-while-subsidizing-animals-that-become-meat/2011/08/22/gIQATFG5IL_story.html

[4] *The Guardian*, 30 April 2013, 'Jobseekers made to carry out bogus psychometric tests'. Byline: Shiv Malik. www.guardian.co.uk/society/2013/apr/30/jobseekers-bogus-psychometric-tests-unemployed

[5] See *Private Eye* No. 1360 21 February — 6 March 2014, p.11.

22. Procurement

[1] See Ian Gilson of Perfect Flow talking about his experience in housing repairs at: ww.vanguard-method.com/v1_lib.php?current=758

23. Risk management

[1] Michael Power, 2007, *Organized uncertainty: designing a world of risk management*, Oxford University Press.

[2] Prime Minister's Strategy Unit, 2002, *Risk: Improving a government's capability to handle risk and uncertainty — Summary Report*. http://webarchive. nationalarchives.gov.uk/+/http:/www.cabinetoffice.gov.uk/media/cabinetoffice/ strategy/assets/su%20risk%20summary.pdf

[3] HM Treasury, October 2004, *The Orange Book: Management of Risk - Principles and Concepts*. www.gov.uk/government/uploads/system/uploads/attachment_ data/file/191513/The_Orange_Book.pdf

[4] National Audit Office, 17 August 2000, *Supporting innovation: Managing risk in government departments*, HC 864 Session 1999-2000. www.nao.org.uk/wp-content/uploads/2000/08/9900864.pdf

[5] See more about HBOS whistleblower Paul Moore at BBC News, Robert Peston blog 11 February 2009 'Why Sir James Crosby resigned': www.bbc.co.uk/blogs/ legacy/thereporters/robertpeston/2009/02/why_crosby_resigned.html

[6] BBC News, 31 October 2011, 'Baby P whistleblower Dr Kim Holt says it is important to speak out': www.bbc.co.uk/news/uk-15522368

[7] John Seddon and Brendan O'Donovan, 2013, 'The Achilles' heel of scale service design in social security administration: The case of the United Kingdom's Universal Credit', *International Social Security Review*, Vol. 66, 1/2013.

24. Lean

[1] James Womack, Daniel Jones and Daniel Roos, 2007, *The Machine That Changed the World*, Simon and Schuster. First published in 1990.

[2] "… Ohno-san never explained his reasons, so the only way to learn was by doing." From 'What I learned from Taiichi Ohno: Interview with Michikazu Tanaka' in Koichi Shimokawa and Takahiro Fujimoto (eds), 2009, *The birth of Lean: conversations with Taiichi Ohno, Eiji Toyoda, and other figures who shaped Toyota management'*, Lean Enterprise Institute, p.57.

[3] For a list of articles written about the various dysfunctional aspects of Lean, see: www.vanguard-method.com/v1_lib.php?current=445

25. IT: – Features over benefits

[1] Whatsthepont blog 'Google Flu, Big Data and The Woozle Effect' Posted on April 6, 2014 http://whatsthepont.com/2014/04/06/google-flu-big-data-and-the-woozle-effect/

[2] *The Observer*, 6 April 2014, 'Google and the flu: how big data will help us make gigantic mistakes'. Byline: John Naughton.

[3] See John Cooney, 'Systems thinking in Planning and Roads' in Middleton, P (ed.) 2010 *Delivering Public Services that Work (Volume 1): Systems Thinking in the Public Sector Case Studies*, Triarchy Press. There are several other examples of the Vanguard Method at work in highways services in the subscriber area of the Vanguard website https://www.vanguard-method.com/content/5/sector/736

[4] 24dash.com, 10 July 2014, 'Lord Freud announces 11 new universal credit trials in speech to LGA conference'. Byline: Jon Land. http://www.24dash.com/news/universal_credit/2014-07-10-Lord-Freud-announces-11-new-universal-credit-trials-in-speech-to-LGA-conference

[5] *The Telegraph*, 10 June 2014, 'Go on the internet - or lose access to government services, Francis Maude tells pensioners'. Byline: Christopher Hope. http://www.telegraph.co.uk/technology/internet/10889563/Go-on-the-internet-or-lose-access-to-government-services-Francis-Maude-tells-pensioners.html

[6] See video by Derek Muller, 10 February 2014, 'Facebook Fraud'. http://www.youtube.com/watch?v=oVfHeWTKjag

Part 5 Change must start in Whitehall

26. Beware economists bearing plausible ideas

[1] See *Local Government Chronicle* 5 November 2008, 'Explained: Keynesian Economics'. Byline: James Illman: "Keynes advocated active state intervention in the marketplace as the best means of stimulating economic growth and promoting stability. Taxation, interest rates and public projects are all central levers of control."

[2] Neoliberalism: "An approach to economics and social studies in which control of economic factors is shifted from the public sector to the private sector. Drawing upon principles of neoclassical economics, neoliberalism suggests that governments reduce deficit spending, limit subsidies, reform tax law to broaden the tax base, remove fixed exchange rates, open up markets to trade by limiting protectionism, privatize state-run businesses, allow private property and back

deregulation." www.investopedia.com/terms/n/neoliberalism.asp

[3] John Maynard Keynes, 1991, *The General Theory of Employment, Interest and Money*, Macmillan, pp.383-384. First published in 1936.

[4] Paul Ormerod, 1994, *The Death of Economics*, Faber and Faber, pp.ix-x.

[5] Steve Keen, 2001, *Debunking Economics: the Naked Emperor of the Social Sciences*, Zed, p.4.

[6] Ha-Joon Chang, 2010, *23 Things They Don't Tell You About Capitalism*, Penguin, pp.62-63.

[7] John Maynard Keynes, *op. cit.*, pp.383-384.

[8] BBC News website, 1 October 2012, 'Mervyn King's economic inspirations' www.bbc.co.uk/news/business-19779659 "[King] credits Hayek with having given economists a valuable warning against hubris. We can't predict the future, [King] says. And we probably can't prevent more crises from happening."

[9] *Financial Times*, 30 May 2014, 'An astonishing record — of complete failure'. Byline: Tim Harford: www.ft.com/cms/s/2/14e323ee-e602-11e3-aeef-00144feabdc0.html

[10] See John Kay, 4 October 2011, 'The Map is Not the Territory: An Essay on the State of Economics': www.johnkay.com/2011/10/04/the-map-is-not-the-territory-an-essay-on-the-state-of-economics

[11] Steve Keen, *op. cit.*, p.4.

[12] John Kay, *op. cit.*

[13] Friedrich Hayek, 11 December 1974, 'Lecture to the memory of Alfred Nobel: The Pretence of Knowledge' www.nobelprize.org/nobel_prizes/economic-sciences/laureates/1974/hayek-lecture.html

[14] Robert Heilbroner, 1953, *The Worldly Philosophers*, Simon and Schuster.

[15] Joan Robinson, 1978, *Contributions to Modern Economics*, Academic Press, p.75.

[16] Julian Le Grand, 2007, *The Other Invisible Hand: Delivering Public Services through Choice and Competition*, Princeton University Press.

[17] *The Observer*, 11 May 2014, 'After the crash, we need a revolution in the way we teach economics'. Byline: Ha-Joon Chang and Jonathan Aldred. www.theguardian.com/business/2014/may/11/after-crash-need-revolution-in-economics-teaching-chang-aldred

[18] Thomas Carlyle, the 19th century Scottish essayist and historian described the emerging discipline of economics as the "dismal science". The term was inspired by T. R. Malthus's gloomy predictions that population would always grow faster than food, dooming mankind to starvation, unending poverty and hardship.

[19] Philip Mirowski, 2013, *Never let a serious crisis go to waste: How Neoliberalism survived the financial meltdown*, Verso, p.24.

[20] *Op. cit.* pp.17-22.

[21] German economist Johann F. von Pfeiffer, 1777, as quoted in Erik S. Reinert, 1999, 'The role of the state in economic growth', *Journal of Economic Studies* Vol. 26 No 4/5, p.315.

27. Whitehall is systemically incapable of doing evidence

[1] Office of the Deputy Prime Minister (ODPM), 2005, *A Systematic Approach to Service Improvement Evaluating Systems Thinking in Housing*, ODPM publications.

[2] Gary Hamel and Polly LaBarre, 'Dispatches From The Front Lines Of Innovation Management', *McKinsey Quarterly*, November 2010.

[3] John Seddon, 2005, *Adult Social Care: a systems analysis and a better way forward.*: www.vanguard-method.com/v1_lib.php?current=515

[4] For example, PricewaterhouseCoopers (PwC) were participants in both the government-sponsored 'Total Place' and DECATS initiatives, whilst Operation QUEST placed a joint KPMG/Home Office consulting team in participating police forces for six months.

[5] Alex Stevens, 2011, 'Telling policy stories: An ethnographic study of the use of evidence in policy-making in the UK', *Journal of Social Policy*, 40 (2). pp.237-256.

[6] Richard Bacon and Christopher Hope, 2013, *Conundrum: Why every government gets things wrong and what we can do about it*, Biteback.

[7] Paul Buxton, 2008, *The Illusion of Control. How Government Targets and Standards Damage Local Government Services*: www.unreasonable-learners. com/wp-content/uploads/2011/03/The-Illusion-of-Control-Article-on-Systems-thinking-application-in-England.pdf

[8] This phrase was neatly summed up by John Kay of the *Financial Times*: "The British government's admirable emphasis on evidence-based policy too often reduces, as it did in this case, to policy-based evidence: information provided supports the conclusions that those who prepare the studies believe policymakers seek." See *Financial Times*, 6 September 2006, 'How the migration

estimates turned out wrong'. Byline: John Kay. www.johnkay.com/2006/09/06/how-the-migration-estimates-turned-out-wrong

28. Getting a focus on purpose

[1] See *Financial Times*, 9 November 2009, 'Fond farewell to a brilliant thinker', Byline: Stefan Stern. http://www.ft.com/cms/s/0/0168c7de-cd7e-11de-8162-00144feabdc0.html#axzz22Hyp8bBK "'All of our problems arise out of doing the wrong thing righter,' [Ackoff] told me. 'The more efficient you are at doing the wrong thing, the wronger you become. It is much better to do the right thing wronger than the wrong thing righter. If you do the right thing wrong and correct it, you get better.'"

Index

About the Author

 John Seddon is a respected and outspoken management thinker and commentator. Trained as an occupational psychologist, he is well known as a speaker and author, and has become an international authority on service organisations in both the public and private sector.

He is Visiting Professor at Hull University Business School and managing director of Vanguard, a consultancy company he formed in 1985 and the inventor of 'The Vanguard Method'. (See Vanguard's website – www.vanguard-method.com – for more information and a library of resources.)

John began his career investigating why major organisational change programmes fail. He learnt from W. Edwards Deming and Taiichi Ohno, in particular, the importance of understanding and managing organisations as systems – an approach that has underpinned his subsequent work.

A long-term critic of the UK's public-sector 'reform programme', John was described by the *Daily Telegraph* as a "reluctant management guru", which seems like the best sort. He won the first Management Innovation Prize for 'Reinventing Leadership' in 2010.

About the Publisher

Triarchy Press is an independent publisher of alternative thinking (altThink) about government, organisations and society at large — as well as the people who participate in them.

Other titles by John Seddon and about the application of The Vanguard Method in practice include:

Systems Thinking in the Public Sector

Delivering Public Services that Work (Volume 1). Systems Thinking in the Public Sector Case Studies

Delivering Public Services that Work (Volume 2). The Vanguard Method in the Public Sector: Case Studies

Other Triarchy Press titles on organisations, leadership, systems thinking and the public sector include:

Ackoff's F/Laws: The Cake

Growing Wings on the Way: Systems Thinking for Messy Situations

Humanising Healthcare

Intelligent Policing

Managers as Designers in the Public Services

Systems Thinking for Curious Managers

The Search for Leadership: An Organisational Perspective

Details of all these titles and others are at:

www.triarchypress.net

Milton Keynes UK
Ingram Content Group UK Ltd.
UKHW020103280923
429401UK00010B/85